COUPLE COMMUNICATION I

TALKING TOGETHER

COUPLE COMMUNICATION I
TALKING TOGETHER

SHEROD MILLER, Ph.D.

ELAM W. NUNNALLY, Ph.D.

DANIEL B. WACKMAN, Ph.D.

ISBN 0-917340-09-4
First Printing, September, 1979
Second Printing, March, 1980
Third Printing, February, 1981
Fourth Printing, September, 1981
Fifth Printing, August, 1982
Sixth Printing, February, 1983
Seventh Printing, January, 1984
Eighth Printing, December, 1984
Ninth Printing, February, 1986
Tenth Printing, July, 1986

Illustrations, Barry Ives
Book Design: Robert Friederichsen
Printing: Printing Arts, Inc.

INTERPERSONAL
COMMUNICATION PROGRAMS

7201 South Broadway
Littleton, Colorado 80122
(303) 794-1764

PREFACE

If you lived for any length of time with both of your parents, no doubt you saw them make decisions together: what food to eat, how much money to spend, what to do with a free evening, what clothes to wear, or maybe just who would walk through a door first. However, the odds are great against having seen your parents talk together about how they typically made decisions or talk openly about any differences they had in their relationship to try to improve it.

Furthermore, until recently, if you and your partner wanted to enhance and develop your relationship, you had no alternative for doing so without declaring that one or both of you were having serious problems and needed a consultant-therapist to help out. And then, if you did see a consultant-therapist while you worked on "your problem," s/he probably spent little or no time teaching you principles and skills for solving future difficulties on your own, without his/her aid. So both at home and elsewhere, limited help was available to assist you in "learning to learn" in your relationship or in enriching your partnership by effectively talking about how you talk.

Now there are alternatives available—Couple Communication is one of them. You don't have to have a problem to qualify either, only a desire to improve the quality of your life with someone important to you, a wish to make something good even better.

ORIGINS OF COUPLE COMMUNICATION

The ideas and skills outlined in *Couple Communication I: Talking Together* were researched and developed by Drs. Sherod Miller, Elam

Nunnally, and Daniel B. Wackman at the University of Minnesota Family Study Center, in cooperation with Minneapolis Family and Children's Service. The approach utilizes modern systems and communication theories, particularly those of William F. Hill, Sidney Jourard, and Virginia Satir, within the broader framework of family development theory pioneered by Reuben Hill. Research studies testing the impact of Couple Communication show that couples related for any length of time—ranging from partners who have recently met to couples married for more than 30 years—can learn the skills taught and, consequently, enrich their relationship.

Since its beginning in 1968, more than 75,000 couples have participated in Couple Communication groups in the United States, and in Canada, Europe and Australia. Over 2,500 instructors have been trained to present Couple Communication. CC instructors come from a variety of backgrounds. Some are teachers, ministers and counselors. Others have had no special professional training in human services but are people who have benefitted a great deal from participating in a Couple Communication group and want to pass the program on to help others. If you are interested in teaching CC and belong to an organization in your community where you could offer the program, see "How To Become A CC Instructor" (page 172 in the Epilogue) and the Information Request Form (on the last page of TALKING TOGETHER) for information on CC instructor materials and training workshops.

COUPLE COMMUNICATION I: TALKING TOGETHER is the text for Couple Communication I. It contains basic concepts and skills which have evolved over the past 12 years, as well as numerous exercises and worksheets for use in Couple Communication groups. For readers interested in other ICP publications and programs related to family and work, see the Epilogue and back cover of TALKING TOGETHER.

ABOUT THE AUTHORS

Sherod Miller is President of Interpersonal Communication Programs, Inc. He lectures widely on the subject of communication and frequently serves as a consultant to major corporations, government and private industry. He was formerly a faculty member in the Department of Medicine at the University of Minnesota, School of Medicine.

Elam W. Nunnally is an Associate Professor, School of Social Welfare, University of Wisconsin - Milwaukee. He is also a marriage and family therapist, and a consultant on family life development. He specializes in family communication and marital interaction in the later years of marriage.

Daniel B. Wackman is Vice-President of Interpersonal Communications programs, Inc. He is also Professor and Director of the Communication Research Division, School of Journalism and Mass Communication, University of Minnesota. His research focuses on the role of family communication in child and adolescent development.

The authors have received awards for development of Couple Communication from the National Council on Family Relations and the Association of Couples for Marriage Enrichment.

ACKNOWLEDGEMENTS

A large network of people have been involved in the growth of Couple Communication I over the past decade. Our mentors from the beginning include:

Reuben Hill, Regents Professor of Family Sociology and former Director of the University of Minnesota Family Study Center;

Earl Beatt, Director of Minneapolis Family and Children Service;

William Fawcett Hill, Professor of Psychology, California State Polytechnic at Pomona, Developer of the Hill Interaction Matrix from which the communication styles framework has evolved;

Sidney Jourard, the late professor of Psychology at the University of Florida;

Virginia Satir, Family Therapist and Educator;

Phyllis Miller, Eeva Nunnally, and Kathy Wackman, our wives and the most significant people in our lives.

Three colleagues and friends—Ramon Corrales, Chet Evenson, and Jim Maddock—have made a number of significant conceptual and practical contributions to the program. Equally important are the CC Instructor Training Associates and CC Instructors who have passed on to us suggestions for improving Couple Communication over the years.

We also want to express our appreciation to those couples who have allowed us to share excerpts of their dialogues with you in this book. Lastly, we want to thank the many couples who have written to tell us about their experiences in Couple Communication and the impact it has had on their lives.

CONTENTS

INTRODUCTION

COUPLE COMMUNICATION

Couple Communication is for partners who want to be in charge of their lives and develop more fulfilling ways of being together. For us, a couple is any two people who have a history and anticipate a future together. This definition obviously includes married couples, but it also includes other pairs, as well, in fact, any two people with more than a transitory relationship.

Couple Communication is based on two beliefs which have been validated many times by people who have participated in the program:

—Sharing yourself with another person is crucial to your growth as an individual. One of the most valuable things you can have for your own personal well-being is a relationship with someone you can both play and talk seriously with; someone you can share your hopes and joys with, as well as your fears and sadness; someone who will listen to you and respond; someone with whom you can relate on many different levels.

—Satisfying relationships are not just found, but rather are actively developed by the partners involved. Further, most partners can learn ways to do this if they are willing to join together in a spirit of good will and commitment.

Merely stating these beliefs does not make them come true. In fact, many pressures in our modern world are making satisfying relationships both more important and more difficult to attain. Examples of stress producing changes abound; double-digit inflation, changes in male-female roles, information explosion, the energy crisis, underemployment, mobility, and multiple-career demands. Many of these stresses impact on relationships in ways that were hardly known even a decade ago. This heightened pressure suggests that, increasingly, couples may have difficulty building a higher-quality relationship, and to do so may take considerable effort and great adaptability.

To support you in strengthening your relationship, Couple Communication offers important tools for dealing with different areas of your daily living: reporting events of the day; planning, scheduling, deciding, affirming and supporting one another; sharing activities and experiences; resolving problems, issues, difficulties; and talking about your hopes for the future. Because these areas vary widely in what is involved, you need to be *flexible* in how you talk together and approach each area. Couple Communication will help you to become more flexible.

What are benefits you can receive from Couple Communication? Couples participating in Couple Communication report a wide range of benefits:

—more ways to talk
—more to talk about
—better understanding of self and partner
—clearer sense of being heard and understood
—boosting of self-worth
—de-escalating of hostility
—new options to fighting
—new and more effective ways of handling day-to-day situations
—better solutions to our major issues
—new ways of being intimate

You and your partner can experience these benefits, too, by adding the skills presented in this book. Let's begin by looking at some basic aspects of Communication.

SOME BASICS ABOUT COMMUNICATION

You may often wish that you and your partner had more time to be together and to talk. In this fast-paced age, time is hard to come by, and often it seems there is just too little of it for the two of you. It is not just how much time you and your partner spend talking that counts, however. Rather, *what* the two of you talk about and, more importantly, *how* the two of you talk are the things that really matter.

WHAT YOU TALK ABOUT

The "what" of your communication—the specific things you talk about with your partner—depends on a host of factors: your interests, beliefs, and values; your point in the life cycle, occupation, family make-up; and various external circumstances, such as recent events, season of the year, even the time of day. There are four directions in which you may focus your talk: external topics, yourself, your partner, or your relationship.

Topic-messages focus on things, events, ideas, places, or on people who are not present and participating in the conversation:

"The kids have been restless today."

"Is there gas in the car?"

Self-messages focus on you as a person, your experiences, thoughts, feelings, and so forth:

"Gee, I've been feeling good lately."

"I'm not sure what I want to do."

Partner-messages focus on your partner as a person, your partner's experiences, thoughts, actions, feelings:

"You really seem worried about that."

"Do you expect to finish today?"

Both self-messages and partner-messages focus on a single person, either you or your partner. In this sense, their focus is *personal,* expressing more personal involvement than topic-messages.

Relationship-messages, the fourth kind of focus, also have a great deal of personal involvement:

"I really feel pleased when you listen to me closely."

"I love you."

Relationship-messages are about you *and* your partner, your joint experiences, your impact on each other, and various aspects of your relationship. They are usually more intimate than either self-messages or partner-messages.

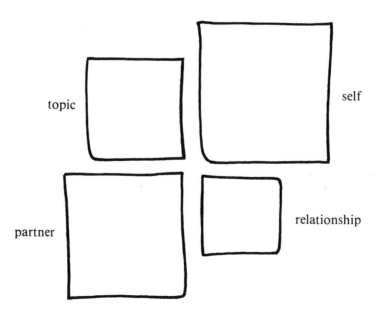

We would like you to stop for a moment and think of some of the conversations you have had recently with your partner. Think about them in terms of *focus.* Are your conversations exclusively topic-focused, or do a substantial number of self-, partner-, and relationship-messages occur, too? When do your conversations include the more person-centered messages: when you're arguing, sharing activities, or making a decision? If your conversations are almost entirely topic-focused, you are probably keeping a lot of life out of your relationship. This is because relationships come alive only when you and your partner get involved with each other. This happens when you focus on yourself, your partner, and especially on the two of you together.

ISSUES

Sharing interests and activities, talking about each person's separate lives and your lives together, and making routine decisions are all important. In addition, however, it is essential that you deal with your issues, too. We will be using the word *issue* frequently and here is our definition: *an issue is anything which concerns one or both partners.* Issues usually require a decision.

Issues are not the same as problems. An issue becomes a problem when it is recurrent and the decisions you and your partner make are consistently unsatisfactory to one or both of you. An issue becomes a problem, too, when you fail to identify it or when you simply refuse to face it and deal with it.

Some couples go to great lengths to avoid dealing with their issues. They do this because they have never learned how to work through issues effectively; they usually end up fighting. These couples simply stop trying. They leave their relationship to chance. This is not necessary. If you identify your issues and deal with them on the basis of shared understanding, you and your partner will be able to create a stronger, more intimate relationship.

Issues develop in a number of different ways. They crop up when circumstances change for you and your partner, for example, when you have a baby, change jobs, move from one place to another. They arise when you or your partner feel some dissatisfaction, perhaps when an old pattern in your relationship isn't working any more. They occur when one of you has broken an expectation and something happens that was not expected. They surface as you and your partner anticipate the future.

The specific issues you and your partner deal with change over time,

but at one time or another, most couples can expect to confront issues
such as these:

identity	productiveness	control
career	goals	together/apartness
housing	death	similarity/difference
values	trust	cooperation/competition
opportunities	sex	boundaries
health	commitment	decision-making
faith	affection	responsibilities

Which of these have you faced in the last year? Is there one that you have
avoided dealing with? Confidence in your ability to deal with issues suc-
cessfully will increase as you develop more effective ways to discuss
them. That's what Couple Communication is mainly about—*how*
couples talk.

HOW YOU TALK

What you and your partner talk about or avoid is important. But even
more important for determining the quality of your relationship is *how*
the two of you talk—the kinds of skills and styles you use. Couples who
are skillful communicators talk in a variety of ways. When an issue arises
for them, they use a communication style which helps them focus directly
on the issue and reach a satisfying decision. Issues do not dominate the
conversations of couples who talk like this, however, because they handle their issues effectively and move on to other things in their lives.

You and your partner can become flexible, skillful communicators,
too, by learning new skills and styles. This book will show you how.

OUTLINE OF TALKING TOGETHER

To help you become a more aware and effective communicator this
book presents *frameworks* for:
- —increasing your self-awareness
- —distinguishing different styles of communication
- —examining your attitude toward yourself and your partner.

It also presents *skills* for:
- —expressing your awareness more clearly, directly, and openly
- —listening accurately to your partner to create understanding
- —building your own and your partner's self-esteem
- —initiating discussion of an issue.

Couple Communication I is divided into four chapters, each presenting a framework and skills related to an important aspect of interpersonal communication. Each chapter includes material to help you understand your communication better and exercises to give you practice with the frameworks and skills. As you progress from chapter to chapter, the frameworks and skills build upon each other, providing the opportunity to learn an integrated approach for improving your communication with your partner.

CHAPTER 1. *TUNING IN TO YOURSELF*

This chapter introduces the Awareness Wheel.™ The Awareness Wheel is the most important learning tool presented in Couple Communication. It is the basis for understanding your own experience and disclosing it to your partner, as well as for tuning into your partner's experience. The Awareness Wheel weaves throughout the book and integrates all of the frameworks and skills presented in Couple Communication. Chapter I also introduces six basic skills for disclosing all the different parts of your experience.

CHAPTER 2. *TUNING IN TO YOUR PARTNER*

This chapter shifts the emphasis from your own awareness and disclosure to your partner's awareness and his/her disclosure. You learn listening skills for helping your partner disclose his/her awareness and the Shared Meaning Process to help you and your partner be more accurate in understanding each other.

CHAPTER 3. *FOUR WAYS OF TALKING*

This chapter introduces the Verbal Communication Styles framework, sensitizing you to differences in how messages can be sent and to the impact different styles have. As these styles become familiar to you, you will be able to move flexibly from one style to another, matching your style with your intentions for each situation.

CHAPTER 4. *COUNTING YOURSELF AND YOUR PARTNER*

This chapter discusses the Counting Framework. It will help you understand how the attitudes you hold about yourself and your partner influence your communication, and how your communication affects these attitudes, too. The chapter shows how one particular attitude—I count me and I count you—helps you and your partner to build esteem and your relationship as well. You can use this framework like a compass to check on whether you are using the skills to head in the direction you really want to go.

HOW TO USE THE BOOK

If you are enrolled in a Couple Communication group, your instructor will give you directions for using the book. If you're not in a group, here's what we suggest: don't read too much at any one time. After reading one chapter, wait several days before reading the next one. Use this time to do exercises—at least two or three—before going on. This provides an opportunity to practice using frameworks and skills from one chapter before learning new materials. Each exercise takes 30 minutes or less.

Chapter 1 is the longest chapter and may require 35 or 40 minutes to read. The other chapters will each require about 20 or 30 minutes to read. As you read, you will notice that some dialogue is in quotation marks and some is not. If the dialogue is in quotes, this indicates *spoken* dialogue; if it is not in quotes, this indicates that a person is *thinking* but not speaking. We have provided large margins in the text to make it easier for you to jot down notes, comments, personal reflections, and the like.

A variety of exercises is included at the end of each chapter. These are labelled to indicate who does them. *Individual* exercises involve only you alone. *Partner* exercises involve you and another person; partner exercises provide an opportunity to practice communication skills, so try to read this book with a partner so the two of you can practice the skills together. *Individual/partner* exercises involve work by you alone to prepare for working together with your partner. *Group* exercises are done in a Couple Communication group. If you are enrolled in a group, leave these exercises for the group.

Each chapter contains a number of exercises, probably more than you will want to do at first. They are organized in the following order: Individual, Individual/Partner, Partner, and Group. Glance through the list and choose those you want to do. It is probably best to choose at least one of each kind.

Each chapter also contains two other forms. The Progress Review can be used to review your progress in learning the various frameworks and skills taught in Couple Communication. Observation Sheets can be used to monitor communication—other group members' during exercises in CC groups or your own and your partner's while listening to tape recordings.

Practice using the skills with others besides your partners'when it seems appropriate to do so. This will help you build increasing competence. You and your partner may find it useful at times to playfully over-use the skills; this helps in learning, too. Another tip passed on to us by participants in Couple Communication groups: develop your skills by using them around smaller and less sensitive issues before tackling really tough issues and decisions.

We would like to sound a note of caution here. You will be pleasantly surprised by what you discover as you and your partner put these frameworks and skills into use. But don't expect your relationship to become completely trouble-free. Life is just not like that. What you *can* count on, however, is this: when the next trouble comes along, you will have the confidence that comes from knowing the two of you were able to handle previous difficulties well.

STAGES OF SKILL-LEARNING

You may find that you go through four distinct stages in learning the skills taught in Couple Communication.

—*Initial learning.* This first stage involves a recognition that there are different ways of communicating than you typically use. Often this leads to a combination of confusion and excitement as you begin to learn the Awareness Wheel and start practicing the self-disclosure skills.

—*Awkward use.* In this stage, you have increased awareness of alternative ways of communicating but frequently experience difficulty in using the new skills. This stage typically occurs when you are beginning to work with the Shared Meaning Process. You feel clumsy and mechanical, and when you use the skills, it just seems like you are not being yourself. At this point, it is sometimes useful just to rant and rave and get these feelings off your chest. During this stage, your spontaneity is reduced.

—*Conscious application.* In this stage, you begin to use the skills more effectively, but you are still self-conscious when you use them. Using the skills feels more comfortable than it did before, however, and you begin to use your own language more in carrying out the skills. Nevertheless, you still feel somewhat mechanical and often have the sense that "this isn't fully me."

—*Natural use.* This final stage typically occurs some time after you have completed your reading of this book and the exercises. It is reached only after a period of time in which you have continued to practice the skills and use them frequently in your daily life. When you reach this stage, you are able to use the skills spontaneously, comfortably, creatively, and congruently to relate to your partner.

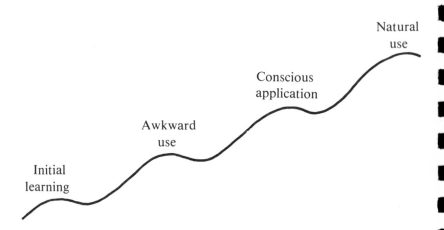

The diagram represents a series of progressions in the development of competence and comfort with the skills. The downtowns in the curve indicate that you are likely to regress toward an earlier stage under stress. For example, when you and your partner deal with an issue involving a great deal of emotion, you are likely to abandon the skills and revert back to old communication patterns. Many people find this frustrating because it is precisely in these situations that they would most like to be able to use the skills.

When this happens to you, don't despair! It is natural for this to occur. Have your fight, or whatever, and then use the skills to talk later, when you feel ready to deal with the issue more constructively. In the natural-use stage, you will less often regress when dealing with tough issues, and you will more frequently experience the glow of satisfaction that comes from effectively dealing with the issues which arise.

USING A TAPE RECORDER

We suggest that you consider tape recording partner exercises. Taping can help you learn more about yourself and your communication. Here are some specific ways to use tapes of exercises:

—As a way of observing your own communication better. It is very difficult to both participate in a discussion and simultaneously monitor your own contribution to the discussion. Tape recording exercises can be very useful for playback and review to hear your own communication.

—As a before/after comparison of your awareness skills.

—As a part of your "family album." Can you imagine having a recording of your grandparents or parents dealing with everyday issues in their lives? Today's technology makes it possible for you and your partner to do this for your family album.

If you decide to make tape recording a part of your experience, record the following discussions for about five minutes each as your first partner exercise:

—Plan something the two of you can do together.

—Talk together about something important in your lives.

Try to keep the discussions to only five minutes. This usually provides an adequate sample of how you and your partner communicate.

Tape recording exercises create a cumulative record of the development of your communication skills. Further, as you replay tapes and listen to yourself, you will increase your skills in applying the frameworks and in observing communication. Using the observation sheets included in each chapter can help you monitor your communication.

JOINING A COUPLE COMMUNICATION GROUP

You can develop your skills more rapidly if you and your partner enroll in a Couple Communication course. A CC course normally is offered over a four-week period, meeting three hours each week. Five to seven couples typically enroll. Groups are led by Certified Instructors.

Courses are offered in churches and synagogues, community colleges, adult education centers and by other organizations interested in promoting personal and relationship growth. If you do not know a Certified Couple Communication Instructor in your community and would like to participate in a CC course, write or call us at:

Couple Communication
Interpersonal Communication Programs
7201 South Broadway
Littleton, Colorado 80122
303-794-1764

We will send you the names of Certified Instructors in your area. A form is provided on the last page of this book for that purpose.

Now, let's move to Chapter 1 and a tool for improving communication—your Awareness Wheel.

SELF AWARENESS

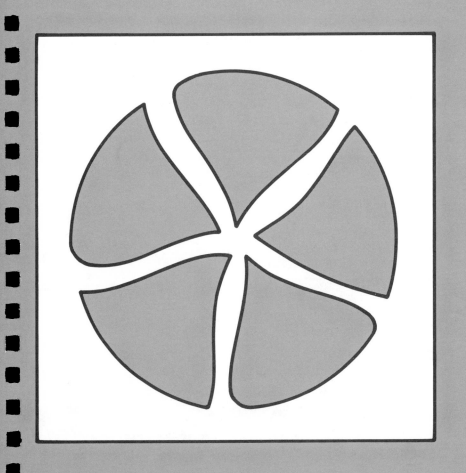

CHAPTER 1

TUNING IN TO YOURSELF

What have you talked about today? An endearing thing your child said to you? Difficulty you were having getting some people to cooperate with you on a project? A good book you are reading? Exciting vacation plans you are making?

Every day most of us talk about these kinds of topics and many more as well because our lives are busy and diverse. The common denominator among all these topics is this: our experience. Your ideas, feelings, and activities provide the content for most of your conversations with others. The reason for this is that all of us talk mainly about our day-to-day world; and even if we are not expert in anything else, each of us is an expert on his/her own experience. So it is natural that you, your partner, your best friend, your child, in fact anyone, talk mainly about their own experiences.

The first step, then, in effective communication is to get in touch with your own experience better. In many situations, we have only limited awareness; we simply miss a lot. Couple Communication begins by teaching you a powerful tool for helping you tune into more facets of yourself. We call this tool the Awareness Wheel. It will help you identify five different parts of your experience in any situation.

The second step in effective communication is learning to express your experience more fully and accurately. Knowing and using specific communication skills can help you describe what's happening with you more adequately. These skills can help you share more of yourself with your partner. We will introduce you to a set of specific skills later in this chapter. Now let's begin with the Awareness Wheel itself.

YOUR AWARENESS WHEEL

There are five parts to your Awareness Wheel. Each part contains important information about your experience. The five parts are your *sensations, interpretations, feelings, intentions,* and *actions.* As you identify each kind of information, you have more complete and helpful information with which to work. To help you grasp the usefulness of the Wheel, let's examine each part more closely.

YOUR INTERPRETATIONS

Interpretations are all the different kinds of meanings you make in your head to help you understand yourself, other people, and situations. They involve the thinking process. Some of the different kinds of interpretations are called:

Impressions	Ideas
Beliefs	Opinions
Conclusions	Expectations
Assumptions	Evaluations

A key point to remember about interpretations is that they are fed by your own unique past, present, and anticipated future experiences. The same goes for your partner. This explains why you and your partner can take the same situation and come up with two very different interpretations, as Bill and Marge did right after Marge introduced Bill to her boss one morning:

Marge: (silently observing and interpreting)
         She's smiling. She's impressed with my man.

Bill: (silently observing and interpreting)
         Her boss is smiling. She's probably wondering how the two of us got together.

In this example, Marge was feeling confident and expected that her boss would like Bill. Bill was feeling ill at ease on the occasion and half-expected not to be liked.

Two people can quite legitimately view the same data differently:

The tank is half empty.   The tank is half full.

Nearly two-thirds of all   More than one-third of marriages
couples never divorce.   end in divorce.

It all depends on where you are coming from. With this in mind, we think it is wise to treat many of our interpretations as tentative, as "maybe's."

Your interpretations are influenced by each of the other parts of your awareness and by other thoughts, as well, especially your beliefs and expectations. The data base for your interpretations, however, lies in one particular part of your awareness—your sensations.

YOUR SENSATIONS

Outside information comes to you through one of your senses — touch, smell, sight, taste, sound. In your first attempts to use the Awareness Wheel, you may confuse sensing with interpreting. The following examples may help you to distinguish between the two:

| I see you smiling. | *sensing* |
| You look happy. | *interpreting* |

| I notice you're frowning. | *sensing* |
| You look worried. | *interpreting* |

| "It's 5:15. I heard you say you'd be back by 4:30." | *sensing* |
| "You're late!" | *interpreting* |

Your senses report raw data. They do the same kind of job that a good news reporter does—observe and describe. But even good journalists often mix sense data with interpretations. For example, a good reporter—using sense data only—might report something like this:

Her eyes widened as she picked up the package. Slowly at first, and then with greater speed she unwrapped and opened the box. She looked at me and smiled.

Now let's notice what a different story it is when the reporter mixes in his own interpretations:

Her eyes widened in surprise as she delightedly picked up the package. Slowly at first, savoring the moment, she began unwrapping it; then, she excitedly ripped off the paper and opened the box. Her warm smile said more than a thousand words.

These two reports illustrate the difference between simply observing something and adding interpretations.

Your senses are the funnel through which all information comes to you. But as you interpret what you see and hear, the data are filtered and transformed; and sometimes you even add to the data. This happens because we all need to "make sense" of what we see and hear.

YOUR FEELINGS

Feelings are the spontaneous, emotional responses you have in a situation. Every day of our lives is filled with a variety of feelings. These often involve a physical sensation in the body:

I'm scared (heart beating fast; breathing fast and shallow; stomach muscles tight).

I feel embarrassed (face and ears feel hot).

I feel contented (breathing deep and slow; muscles in face, neck, and shoulders are relaxed).

To help you identify some typical feelings or emotions, here is a partial list of feelings that people experience:

pleased	lonely	sad
calm	elated	discontented
satisfied	hesitant	anxious
bored	eager	discouraged
jubilant	angry	amazed
confused	joyous	amused
excited	frustrated	upset

One of the difficult things about identifying feelings is that they often occur in combination. You may feel irritated, cautious, and surprised, all at the same time. To complicate matters further, the intensity of feelings varies. That is, you may feel very relaxed, mildly relaxed, or barely relaxed. Finally, your multiple feelings may be in conflict. Remember the last time someone you cared about was very late for an appointment with you, or late coming home? You probably felt both angry and relieved —even joyous—at their safe arrival.

Most of us have had the experience of becoming aware much later—days later sometimes—of how we were really feeling during a particular interaction. It might have been a warm, affectionate feeling or a hurt, angry feeling, or even a sexy feeling. And you think, regretfully, of how differently you might have acted if you had been aware of just what you were feeling at the time. Experiences such as this highlight the value of bringing feelings into your immediate awareness.

Feelings serve as a barometer. They alert you to what is going on and help you to understand your reaction to a situation. It's natural for you to have feelings. They do not have to be apologized for, justified, or explained. You are human, so you feel.

Feelings cannot be controlled by ignoring them or done away with by denying them. But they may change as you reassess sense data and the interpretations you have made. This is important because it means that you can sometimes change how you feel about a situation.

Here are some ways in which you can heighten awareness of your feelings:

—Notice the cues your body gives you: heartbeat, sweating, skin flush, breathing, swallowing, warm or cold sensations, tightening or relaxing of various muscles.

—Notice how you are responding to someone, e.g., smiling, eye contact, posture, voice tone.

—Notice your intentions: for example, if you want to give someone a gift, then the chances are you are feeling warm and loving or perhaps grateful.

—Silently ask yourself, What am I feeling right now?

—Try to tell your feelings to your partner.

Stop for a moment and think about this: How do you usually know what you are feeling?

YOUR INTENTIONS

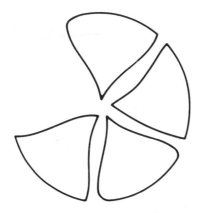

Intentions are what you want—ways you want to be or things you want to do in a situation. Intentions typically involve an attitude of moving toward or away from something.

Intentions may be long range (I'd like to live on a lake some day) or short range (I want five minutes by myself now). They may be broad goals (I want financial security) or narrow objectives (I would like to swim a mile a day within three months).

Intentions can be unpleasant, as well as pleasant, so sometimes they are hard to identify. Here are some common intentions:

to persuade	to understand	to be friendly
to clarify	to help	to share
to praise	to accept	to play
to hurt	to demand	to explore
to conceal	to disregard	to reject
to ignore	to avoid	to exploit

As with feelings, intentions are often held in combination, and one intention may conflict with another: Part of me wants to be with you, and part of me wants to be by myself right now. They vary in intensity too: on a scale of one to ten, your desire for a pizza may be a nine on Monday and only a two on Wednesday.

Sometimes you may try to push an intention right out of your awareness when you feel ashamed or guilty about it, for example, wanting to get even with your partner. But it's most important at such times to maintain awareness so that you can *choose* what you will do. Your wants are the springboard for action. If you don't even know you are *on* a springboard, you may find yourself in deep water before you know it.

Think of your intentions as organizers. Probably the most important function of intentions is to help you review alternative actions, things you want and don't want to do. For example, suppose you want your partner to feel appreciated. Identifying that intention can help you to find possible actions to support your intention, such as:

—listening attentively to partner;

—arranging something special for the two of you;

—offering to do some chore that your partner usually handles.

Here are some ways in which you can heighten awareness of your intentions:

—Silently ask yourself, What do I want right now.

—Directly disclose your wants to your partner.

—Notice your actions and realize that there was something you wanted for yourself that the action seemed likely to provide.

Believe your behavior! Your actions provide excellent clues to your intentions.

YOUR ACTIONS

The action part of your Awareness Wheel includes what you are doing now, what you did or were doing earlier, and what you will be doing later.

I spent all day Saturday doing laundry and cleaning house.	*past action*
I'm doing the laundry.	*present action*
Next Saturday I'm not doing any housework! I'm going to play tennis and relax!	*future action*

Future actions are often confused with intentions. The difference is that here we are talking about what I *will* do—a commitment to action. Intentions do not express a definite commitment to act.

It's hard to be aware of all your actions because so much is happening at one time. Constant self-monitoring would interfere with spontaneity anyway. But when you need it, your partner's responses to you provide cues to help you identify your own actions. Your actions are the raw data that your partner's senses take in and respond to. Being aware of your actions can help you understand your partner's reactions to you. Here are some everyday examples:

"You're doing 65."	You didn't realize you were driving faster than the speed limit.
"You always smile when you say 'good morning.' I like that."	You weren't aware you smiled.

It can be especially useful to you to take a look at some of your behavior patterns. Being aware of the actions which you repeat in certain kinds of situations will help you change them if you want to. One of the authors, for example, drops his voice to a near whisper at the end of a sentence, when not confident about what he is saying. Another has a tendency to say "no" to any request before really thinking about it.

Think about your own patterns of behavior. Can you identify some of them?

PUTTING YOUR AWARENESS WHEEL TOGETHER

Your Awareness Wheel is always about something. The something may be an issue, a situation, or a decision. To make this clear, we add a sixth part to the Wheel — a hub. This indicates that your awareness revolves around the issue, situation or decision which concerns you. Some common examples are:

buying a house   changing a job
care of children   sex
handling disagreements   finding time for one another

Probably the most important use of the Awareness Wheel is to carefully and thoroughly sort out an issue for yourself. This gives you a firm grasp on what the issue is all about and greater knowledge of where you are coming from. Here is an example of what we mean.

In the past few weeks Rod and Nancy have had a series of disagreements about how to deal with their thirteen-year-old daughter, Sherie. Before re-opening the discussion with Nancy, Rod takes some time by himself to sit quietly, breathe deeply, relax and focus upon his awareness around the issue. Here is what comes into his awareness:

All of our arguments seemed to be about how to discipline Sherie when she didn't do something she was supposed to do.	*interpretation*
Nancy scowled or disagreed with me when I got after Sherie for not feeding the pets, for not cleaning her room, and for not helping Nancy with the dishes.	*sensation*
Nancy told me last week that I'm too hard on Sherie.	*sensation*
Nancy thinks I expect too much of Sherie.	*interpretation*
I heard Sherie complain to Nancy that I'm "on her back" all the time.	*sensation*
I hate disagreeing with Nancy about Sherie. It's kind of scary to find us so apart on this. It's confusing, too.	*feeling*
I didn't expect Nancy to act like Sherie needs rescuing from me.	*interpretation*
I'd like to pay Nancy back for that! But I don't want to be childish either. Mostly, I'd like to get this worked out.	*intentions*
I'll talk to Nancy and try to understand her point of view.	*action-future*
I really may have unrealistic expectations of a teenager.	*interpretation*
I'm going to be completely candid with Nancy about my view of it.	*action-future*
I have yelled at Sherie about different things and spoken to her sarcastically.	*action-past*

I feel sort of guilty about that; I wouldn't talk to a friend like that.	*feeling/ interpretation*
I'm going to talk to Sherie, too, to see if she really has a point to make about pressure I'm putting on her.	*action-future*
But I don't want to make a doormat of myself.	*intention*
I think I've got a handle on this now.	*interpretation*
I feel relieved—a lot more hopeful.	*feeling*

There are three things we would like you to notice in this example. First, the different parts of the wheel are connected so that one part of awareness naturally leads to another. Second, different parts come in and out of focus in a variety of sequences. Rod moves from interpretation to sensation, to feeling, back to interpretation, to intention, back to interpretation, to action, and so on. Third, after "spinning" his Awareness Wheel, Rod now understands himself and his situation much better. He is in a much better position to talk constructively with Nancy and Sherie. Using the Awareness Wheel in this careful and thorough way is a good way to prepare for the discussion of an issue.

Another major use of the Awareness Wheel is to maintain high awareness of immediate experience. Notice how Nancy uses her wheel:

I'm starting to feel edgy *(feeling)*. Rod just looked into Sherie's room *(sensation)*, and he must have seen her clothes lying on the floor *(interpretation)*. He's probably going to get after her again *(interpretation)*. I'm going to talk to Rod about this *(action-future)*, but I don't want an argument *(intention)*.

Nancy pays attention to her "edgy" feeling and makes connections with her other awareness parts. Now she can act with high awareness and choice. This is important to anyone who wants to be responsible for him/herself.

PATTERNS OF AWARENESS

Most people are more in touch with one dimension of their Awareness Wheel than with others. When they begin to tune in to their awareness, one part usually comes first. Let's contrast Betty and Jean's patterns:

Betty usually was first aware of her feelings—I love it here; it seems so free! From there she often moves to intentions—I want to just stand here and enjoy it all. Interpretations and sense data would come into awareness later.

Jean usually becomes aware of her intentions first—I want to get away from you. From there she usually moves to interpretations and feelings— When you're as mad as you are, I feel anxious.

Jean is like Betty in that sense data often come into awareness after the other parts.

LIMITED AWARENESS

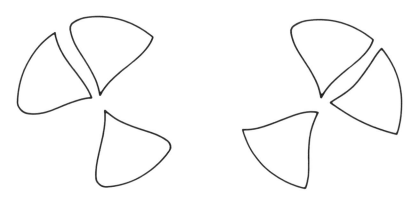

In addition to having a most favored awareness dimension, most people have a least favored dimension, a part of awareness that usually comes last or not at all. You have *limited awareness* in a situation when part of your awareness is left out; the part that's left out is typically your least favored part. Many people leave out two or even three dimensions regularly. In the examples above, Betty and Jean are more likely to leave out awareness of actions than any other part. And Jean might have to stop and think hard to recall the sense data—what she saw or heard from her partner—that led her to conclude he was angry.

Limited awareness occurs (1) when you *don't pay attention* to one or more parts of your experience, or (2) when you *deny* one aspect of your experience, or (3) when you *focus* your attention so strongly on one dimension that all others are left on the sideline. Here are some illustrations of what we mean:

> Bob and Lynn had just finished supper. Lynn asked Bob if he would mind going grocery shopping with her. "Not at all, let's go," Bob replied. But in the course of their shopping, Bob was irritable and made a couple of petty, critical remarks. The shopping trip was unpleasant for both of them.

Here, Bob failed to pay attention to an intention—wanting time for himself that evening to finish a report. During the trip he began to feel anxious about the report, and his unacknowledged anxiety surfaced in the form of irritation.

> Dean asked Jill if she would mind too much if they skipped the party at their friends since he had to get up very early the next morning. Hesitating only a fraction, Jill replied (in a tired, flat tone of voice),

"Sure, that's fine; we can go some other time." She was quiet and "down" the rest of the evening. When Dean commented on Jill's mood, she replied that nothing was the matter, that she was just tired.

In this instance, Jill's feelings of disappointment barely surfaced before she squashed them. But the feelings did not just go away. Even though Jill was not conscious of them, they interfered with her making a choice for herself about the evening and resulted in some confusing messages to Dean.

Jim was concentrating on his model plane, aware only of the plane and what he was doing with it. He didn't hear his son's stereo, or the phone ringing, or his wife saying that she was going somewhere. Later he became angry at his wife for leaving without telling him she was going.

Here, Jim's concentration serves a useful purpose of permitting him to work very productively on the model. Often such concentration leads to no problem, but on this occasion it did. Jim actually did hear his wife say she was going out, and he nodded in reply, but his concentration was so intense that he never truly registered what he had heard from her.

In some situations, limited awareness does not matter much, such as on a tension-free sociable occasion. But in other situations limited awareness has unpleasant consequences:

—The hidden part of your experiences may influence you without your realizing it, as did Bob's unnoticed wish to work on his report and Jill's squashed feelings of disappointment about going out.

—You may send your partner misleading messages as Jill did. Her words gave one message; her face and general manner gave another message.

—You miss information about your experience and your situation, and this can limit your choices.

A sure sign that you are experiencing limited awareness is a mismatch between awareness dimensions, for example, when something you *want* does not match what you *do:*

You want to get up early on Saturday, but you turn the alarm off and go back to sleep.

You want to let your partner know how much s/he means to you, but you say nothing.

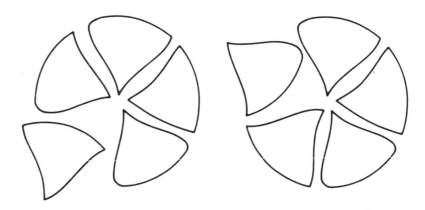

The incongruency, or mismatch, between dimensions lets you know that some hidden part is playing an important role—a wish for more sleep; a wish to avoid being vulnerable.

Sometimes incongruency shows up in your communication with your partner, a mismatch between *what* you say and *how* you say it:

> "I'm happy for you about your promotion, Karen." (spoken solemnly, flat tone of voice, no eye contact)

In this situation Frank was truly happy for Karen that she got her promotion. He knew how much it meant to her. But he was *also* feeling sad because he anticipated that he would have less time with her after her change of job assignment. He told her about the happy feeling but the sad feeling came out in his tone of voice and manner. This could be puzzling and confusing for Karen.

When you notice an incongruency in your communication or in your overt behavior, treat this as important information. This is a signal to you that somewhere outside your immediate awareness there is a feeling or intention that conflicts with other feelings or intentions. Centering your attention can help you to get hold of this missing part of your awareness.

Stop for a moment now and think about yourself. Do you have a typical pattern of limited awareness? With your partner? With other people? Which dimension or dimensions do you leave out? In what situations does limited awareness typically occur for you?

Self-awareness can be increased, and you can develop full awareness. But full awareness does not mean all parts are equal: it just means there is some balance between them. You still are likely to have a strongest dimension in your wheel. We know that it will not be easy to change your old patterns of awareness. Try to think of overcoming your limited awareness as an expansion, stretching yourself to develop new capabilities. Filling your Awareness Wheel out carefully and completely can help you develop these new capacities. So can disclosing yourself more fully to your partner. Self-awareness and self-disclosure are closely related.

SHARING YOUR AWARENESS

Filling out your Awareness Wheel is an important step toward effective communication. It increases your *understanding*. It opens up *choices*. But even with your high self-awareness and greater choice, there is still the possibility of sharing yourself either well or poorly, depending on the communication skills you use. So we come to the next step in effective communication—the use of disclosure skills.

When you and your partner are talking together you are sharing one or more parts of your Awareness Wheels, and you are making:

sense statements
interpretive statements
feeling statements
intention statements
action statements

We refer to each of these as a specific communication skill. But they can be called *skills* only when they are used along with the first self-disclosure skill: Speaking for Self.

SPEAKING FOR SELF

When you speak for yourself, you report your own sensations, thoughts, feelings, intentions, and actions in a way that clearly says that you do, indeed, *own* them. You identify yourself as being at the center of your awareness. You are the person who is alive to, aware of, and responsible for your own experience. Notice how the statements below identify the speaker. There is no question about whose experience it is.

"I want more time to think about it."

"Your decision really pleases me."

"I think you'd get better results with Billy by praising him more often."

"Here's my idea."

"I understood you to say that you planned to go."

As the examples show, in speaking for self you use words that refer to yourself a lot—I, me, my, mine and so forth. These words show clearly you are disclosing your own experience. But they also make it clear you are not speaking for someone else. Instead, speaking for self gives the other person room to experience and report his/her own Awareness Wheel.

If you do speak for your partner, making *over-responsible* you-statements, you may sound like this:

"That's not what you really think!"

"You're not listening."

"Now you're angry."

"We would like to come to your party."

"You heard me the first time."

When you speak for another person you act as if you know better than s/he does what s/he is experiencing. If you frequently speak for your partner, s/he may feel hemmed in, trapped, like s/he has too little room for self. Can you remember how you felt the last time someone spoke for you this way?

Sometimes, when you fail to speak for self, you wind up speaking for no one, making *under-responsible* statements which may sound like one of these:

"It's nice to know you're interested."

"One would think it's possible."

"Some people think this is a good way to do it."

"Women feel stronger about that than men."

Under-responsible statements speak for no one; rather they substitute "it," "most people," or "one" for "I." Sometimes they include no pronoun or reference at all. The opinions, intentions, or feelings of the under-responsible speaker can only be guessed at because they are told in such a cautious, uncommitted way. The speaker does not appear to value them enough to claim them directly. In time, if s/he continually talks in an under-responsible way, s/he may succeed in getting others to devalue him/herself too.

MAKING SENSE STATEMENTS

Making sense statements is the skill of describing what you see, hear, touch, taste, and smell. It's the skill of reporting the sense data you take in. The essence of making a sense statement is being specific about time, place, and action or behavior. The more specific the sense statement, the more useful it usually is. Here are some examples:

"Yesterday, when you first got up..."   *specific about time*

"At the park today, I saw you..."   *specific about place*

"Just as you began to respond to my question, I saw you pause and look down, and then I heard you say..."   *specific about other's actions*

Sense statements help your partner orient him/herself to your experience. And in a very real way they are an aid to you in "making sense" out of your own experience too. Sense statements give both your partner and yourself data to answer questions about "what," "where," "when," "how," and "who."

Sense statements are used in the process of *documenting*. By documenting we mean providing the descriptive data that lead to your interpretation. Let's hear how documenting worked with John and Carol:

Smoothing down his lapels, John turned to Carol and said, "I don't think you like my new suit."

"That's not true!" Carol replied. "What makes you say that?"

"When I tried it on, you were very quiet and you were grinning." *(Documenting)*

Carol said, "Wait a second. I was quiet because I was thinking about how nice you looked. I guess I was grinning because I'm proud of you."

Documenting gives your partner a much clearer idea of what you are referring to specifically. It puts the data you are operating from "on the table." This gives your partner a chance to tell you how s/he's responding to the same data.

One word of caution: It's a misuse of documenting to try to prove a point with data, to try to force your partner to see it your way. But used as we have described in this section, documenting can be extremely helpful in increasing understanding between partners.

MAKING INTERPRETIVE STATEMENTS

Interpretations are the most common type of statement because people are saying what they think all the time. Since this is the case, everybody must be pretty good at making them, right? Wrong. Too often interpretations are made sloppily, in such a careless manner that the listener is unclear or even confused about what is meant. It does not have to be this way, though; interpretive statements can be made skillfully—clear, concise, and focused.

Here are some examples of interpretive statements:

"I think it's time to stop."

"I think you'd enjoy it."

"It seems likely to me."

Notice, all these statements are undocumented interpretations. In a conversation, some of them might require documentation with sense statements to help your partner see how you arrived at your interpretation.

Documenting is especially important when you offer your partner feedback about his/her behavior and its impact on you. Let's contrast documented and undocumented feedback:

undocumented	*documented*
"You're not listening to me."	"I see you looking at the T.V., and I don't think you can do that and listen to me too."
"You don't want to visit my folks."	"Your voice sounded so sad and lifeless when you agreed to go. I can't believe you really want to visit my folks. Do you?"

Notice in the undocumented examples how the speaker slips into speaking for the partner. In the documented examples, the speaker speaks for self and gives specific information about how his/her partner is coming across but does not speak for the partner. By disclosing the sensory data the speaker disclaims any sort of private pipeline to his/her partner's insides and leaves room for the partner to either accept the feedback or respond with a correction. In this way you can let your partner know your thoughts about what is going on inside him/her without speaking for your partner. You do this by:

—Speaking for self;

—Staying tentative about your impressions;

—Sharing your data fully.

MAKING FEELING STATEMENTS

When you make a feeling statement you use words to tell your partner what your feeling is. You make your inner, emotional experience more conscious to yourself and more available to your partner.

You can tell your feelings directly and clearly by simply saying, "I feel...," or "I'm...," as in the following examples:

"I'm really happy about the way we worked together redecorating this place!"

"I'm worried about Billy's homework."

"I'm surprised you thought that way about it."

Even mixed feelings can be expressed simply and directly. When Ron suggested to Pat that they take their vacation in Hawaii, Pat had some very mixed feelings: "Wow, I'd love to. I'm getting excited just thinking about it. But I'm kinda worried about whether we can afford it. Do you think we can?"

A common difficulty people have in making feeling statements is that they substitute opinions, evaluations, or questions for statements of feeling:

"We have good times together" *instead of* "I feel happy when I'm with you."

"You shouldn't work late so often" *instead of* "I'm lonely for you; I miss you."

How about your own expression of feelings? Can you think of some situations when you have disclosed your feelings indirectly with opinions, evaluations, or questions? How could you have translated them into feeling statements?

Sharing feelings seems very personal, a more intimate experience than sharing thoughts. In fact, many of us were brought up to keep feelings hidden behind a door marked "Private." Disclosing feelings may seem risky to you, as if you leave yourself vulnerable to rejection or being laughed at. But when you share feelings with your partner you also become open to connecting at a deeper and more meaningful level.

Sometimes you express your feelings through nonverbal action. You may do this directly (kissing, laughing, crying, storming around) or symbolically (buying a gift, staying away). Expressing feelings through action often has high impact on your partner, but *words* may be needed to clarify what it is exactly that you are feeling. Take crying, for example. Do the tears express sadness, disappointment, anger, or relief? Does your gift express affection, appreciation, or perhaps guilt? When you want your partner to know exactly what you are feeling, make verbal feeling statements.

MAKING INTENTION STATEMENTS

Intention statements let you partner know what you want. You provide your partner with information about what you would like for yourself or what you want to do. When you make intention statements you use words such as, "I want...," "I don't want...," "I'd like...," "I intend...." Here are some examples:

"I want to be with you today, but I don't want to spend all our time doing chores."

"I'd like to tell you about something interesting that happened to me today."

As with feelings, intentions can be in conflict. But these conflicting intentions can be disclosed clearly if you express all the intentions you have:

"I'd like to be alone with you tonight, but I'd like to visit my folks, too, because it's my brother's birthday."

A common difficulty people have in making intention statements, as with feeling statements, is the habit of substituting directives, evaluations, or questions for statements of intention:

"You shouldn't do that" *instead of* "I want you to stop that."

"Don't you think that's too expensive?" *when you mean* "I think that's too expensive."

With practice, anyone can learn to directly state their wants with clear intention statements.

When you do not express your intentions directly you may leave your partner unclear about your desires. Listen to this:

"Well, I know you'd like to play tennis this afternoon, and I might be able to do it. I suppose I could. If we don't today, maybe we can next week."

Will they ever get together on the tennis court? Who knows! The key words here are "might," "could," "maybe." These are spongy words that do not state directly what you want.

Note the difference when intentions are stated clearly:

> "Well, I know you'd like to play tennis this aftenoon, and I'd like that, too. I think I can, although I've got a lot of work to do. Call me about 3:00. Okay? If I can't get away today, I'd sure like to play tomorrow."

This couple is much more likely to get it together, both on the tennis court and in their relationship.

MAKING ACTION STATEMENTS

An action statement reports on your behavior in a simple, descriptive way. Action statements refer to your own past, current, or future actions:

> "I tried to call you earlier."

> "I'm listening."

> "I'll take care of it."

Are action statements really necessary? Isn't your behavior obvious to everyone? Well, no, as a matter of fact, it is not always clear. Consider the action statement, "I was thinking about some stuff at the office and didn't hear you." The only thing obvious to my partner was that I was sitting motionless, staring off into space. S/he may or may not be able to guess that the reason I was not listening was my preoccupation with thoughts about the office. My action statement makes guessing unnecessary.

Furthermore, action statements let people know that you are aware of your own behavior. For example, when I tell my partner, "I interrupted you," this lets my partner know that I care about the impact of my action on him/her. It is a way of saying, "You're important to me."

Finally, action statements are a way of letting your partner know the meaning which you have for your own behavior: "I'm yawning because I didn't get to bed till after 2:00. I'm not bored or anything."

Action statements about the future are particularly important because they involve a *commitment* to doing or not doing something. What a difference between saying, "I can...." "I could...," or "I might...," and clearly committing yourself to an action by saying, "I *will....*" You make a future action statement to let your partner know just what s/he can expect from you. It also provides a check on whether or not you take responsibility for fulfilling your commitments. By carrying out the action, you can demonstrate that you live up to your commitments—and this increases trust between you and your partner.

MULTIPLE-PART STATEMENTS

 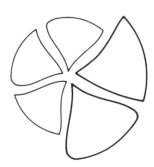

The key to completeness and clarity in disclosing your experience is to put all the skills together during a conversation so that you express all parts of your Awareness Wheel. It is not necessary to do so in a single statement, however. In fact, if you try, your statements are likely to get long, complicated, and confusing. Instead, just put two or three parts of your wheel together. This makes for richness and depth in your communication.

Documented interpretations are one kind of two-part message you are familiar with already. Here are other types of two-part messages:

"I'm excited about my new job *(feeling)*. I want to start as soon as I can" *(intention)*.

"I wasn't sure I wanted to go *(intention)*. That's why I hadn't said anything about it since the time I first mentioned it" *(action-past)*.

Three-part messages are even more complete:

"I'm excited about my new job. I want to start as soon as I can. I think it will open new career opportunities for me" *(interpretation)*.

"I wasn't sure I wanted to go. That's why I hadn't said anything about it since the time I first mentioned it. I was afraid to say anything because I didn't want to disappoint you" *(feeling/intention)*.

Two-part and three-part messages are not just more complete; they are clearer too. The second and third parts provide more context for understanding the first part. Often they show your partner how you see the parts of your awareness fitting together. Multiple-part statements are a good way to help your partner understand you better.

KEY IDEAS FROM CHAPTER 1

1. Self-awareness is the process of tuning in to your experience. The Awareness Wheel is a tool you can use for increasing self-awareness.

2. Your Awareness Wheel has five different kinds of self-information:

    Sensations
    Interpretations
    Feelings
    Intentions
    Actions

3. Each person has his/her own pattern of awareness, with more favored and less favored awareness dimensions.

4. Increasing your self-awareness increases your choices.

5. Disclosing your self-awareness involves skills:

    Speaking for self
    Making sense statements
    Making interpretive statements
    Making feeling statements
    Making intention statements
    Making action statements

6. Multiple-part statements add clarity to your communication.

THINKING BACK ON YOUR DAY   Individual

This exercise provides practice in using your Awareness Wheel. Think back to something that happened today—interesting, puzzling, bothersome, etc. Ask yourself these questions and answer them in the space provided.

a.   What did I *sense*—see, hear, smell, etc.?

b.   What did I *think*—what interpretations did I make?

c.   What did I *feel*—what was my emotional reaction?

d.   What were my *intentions*—what did I want, if anything?

e.   What did I *do*—verbally and/or nonverbally?

YOUR FEELINGS   Individual

Listed below are feelings (emotions) that most people have in different situations. The purpose of this exercise is to help you identify your feelings and become more aware about how you do or do not share them.

For each feeling, draw two X-s and two lines. Let a dotted line represent how often you are *aware* of experiencing the feeling and a solid line represent how often you *disclose* the feeling to your partner.

Notice the variation between *awareness* and *disclosure.* For example, I may frequently be aware of feeling confident but rarely express this to my partner:

                    never   rarely   sometimes   frequently
confident. . . . . .X (awareness)
                    _____X (disclosure)

Whatever you experience, we hope you'll be honest with yourself and accept your feelings as your own. We find it more useful to think of feelings in terms of what *is,* rather than what should or should not be, or what is good or bad.

FEELINGS	never	rarely	sometimes	frequently	FEELINGS	never	rarely	sometimes	frequently
stubborn					surprised				
loving					sad				
angry					excited				
contented					fearful				
jealous					bored				
disappointed					proud				
grateful					depressed				
embarrassed					shy				
cautious					lonely				
daring					tender				
confused					pleased				
anxious					guilty				
sexy					appreciative				
frustrated					happy				

Ideas for this exercise are adapted from "An Emotional Inventory," *Agape,* January, 1976, pp. 28-29.

REFLECTING ON AN ISSUE   Individual

Here is an exercise to give you practice in heightening self-awareness about a current concern of yours. First, sit back and let yourself relax for a moment. Next, let a current personal concern (issue, situation) come into your mind—dissatisfaction with work, how to spend your money, difficulty relating to your partner, etc. Write the concern in the hub of the Wheel.

Now begin to free associate and write down key words or phrases as they occur to you under the five different dimensions of your Awareness Wheel. Don't censor yourself—let your experience flow and record it under the appropriate dimension. (If you have difficulty deciding which dimension to list your awareness under, that's okay. This will help you discover what parts of the Wheel you do not understand fully.)

You will become more skilled using this tool as time passes. See how much information you can generate about yourself and the issue. See where confusion or low awareness exists. Do not try to resolve or deal with the issue—just describe it. This is an exercise in heightening your own self-awareness.

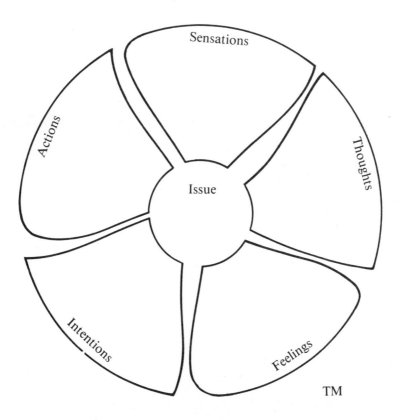

LISTENING TO CONVERSATIONS   Individual

Listen to conversations around you at home, work, or with friends or strangers. What types of statements are typical in these conversations—sense   statements, interpretive statements (opinions, evaluations, etc.), feeling statements, intention statements, action statements? What types of statements are usually left out?

TWENTY-FIVE WORDS OR LESS   Individual

Send your partner two telegrams or notes this week expressing *all* dimensions of the Awareness Wheel in 25 words or less.

SELF-DISCLOSURE SKILLS QUIZ   Individual

The fifteen statements below represent each of the five dimensions of the Awareness Wheel and illustrate five self-disclosure skills. Can you identify which skill each statement represents?

a) sense statement   d) intention statement
b) interpretive statement   e) action statement
c) feeling statement

Answer

1. I'd like to get some time to talk about our vacation coming up.   _____

2. I get angry and frustrated when you don't follow through with what you say you'll do.   _____

3. I don't think she cares.   _____

4. Wow, I was excited to hear from you.   _____

5. I'll bet you don't know what I want from you.   _____

6. I didn't go last week.   _____

7. I notice you're leaning back in your chair, not smiling.   _____

8. I think you misunderstood her.   _____

9. I'll call Jim tomorrow morning.   _____

10. I'm confident about it.   _____

11. I'd like to let you know what I'm thinking.   _____

12. I smell your perfume.   _____

13. I want to start soon.   _____

14. I'm listening.   _____

15. Yesterday at supper, I heard you say you were interested in going.   _____

Answers can be found on page 174

PATTERNS OF AWARENESS

Individual/Partner

Pick two of the following three situations: on your job, with your partner, and with children or friends. In each situation, think about what part of your Awareness Wheel you are aware of first, second, and so forth. Number the part of the Wheel from 1 to 5 (first to last).

On your job   With partner   With children or friends

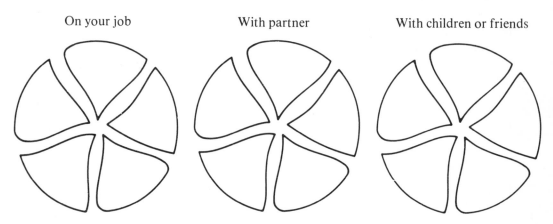

After tracing your awareness for each situation, compare the two patterns. Did you enter your Awareness Wheel in the same place each time, or in different places? Did you move around your Wheel in the same sequence, or did you have different sequences? Were you more strongly aware of one or two dimensions than the others? Did you touch each part of the Wheel in each situation, or did you consistently leave out one or two parts? Do you have a consistent awareness pattern?

Next, compare your Wheels with your partner's to see how similar or different the two of you are in how you experience awareness in situations.

YOUR SKILL PRACTICE
Partner

Talk with your partner about how well you are doing in practicing the skill you chose for this week. Pay particular attention to documenting times when you used the skill well and times when you could have used it but didn't. You might also want to talk about how you have used the skills with other people, such as children, friends, colleagues at work.

WE/YOU/I
Partner

Pick a topic and discuss it for three minutes with your partner, beginning each sentence with the pronoun "we." Next, continue discussing the same topic, or pick a new one, and discuss it for three minutes, beginning each sentence with "you." Finally, continue with the same topic or pick a new one and discuss it for three minutes, beginning each sentence with "I."

Tape Recording

It is helpful to tape record each of these discussions, then listen to them after you have finished all three discussions. Pay attention to the different impact the words "we," "you," and "I" have on the discussion.

SHARING A PERSONAL EXPERIENCE
Partner

Share some meaningful experience you have had in the last few days. Try to use your Awareness Wheel and all of the self-disclosure skills as you tell your partner about the experience. After you are finished, your partner shares his/her experience with you.

COMMUNICATION SKILLS CHECKLIST

Group

Listed below are the first six skills taught in Couple Communication. Without consulting your partner, put an X on the line next to the skill you would be willing to practice during the next week. Next, put an X on the line next to the skill you would like your partner to practice during the week.

When you compare your check list with your partner's, you may use your partner as a consultant. But be sure to choose a skill you really want to practice during the next week.

		Self	Partner
1.	Speaking for self	____	____
2.	Making sense statements	____	____
3.	Making interpretive statements	____	____
4.	Making feeling statements	____	____
5.	Making intention statements	____	____
6.	Making action statements	____	____

PROGRESS REVIEW

Here's an exercise to help you assess your own progress in learning communication skills. Rate yourself by placing an X in the blank to indicate where you presently are in the process of learning each of the skills, processes, and frameworks presented in Chapter 1. This review is for your own purposes; *share* it with your partner if you wish.

	Initial Learning	Awkward Use	Conscious Application	Natural Use
SKILLS				
Speaking for self				
Making sense statements				
Making interpretive statements				
Making feeling statements				
Making intention statements				
Making action statements				
PROCESS				
Documenting interpretations with data				
FRAMEWORKS				
The Awareness Wheel				

TAPE OBSERVATION SHEET

This sheet is provided to help you listen to tapes you and your partner made and monitor your own behavior. As you are listening to a tape, jot down words or phrases that will help you document when you used particular skills or behaviors.

Tape 1

Speaking for
self

Speaking for
other

Sense
statements

Interpretive
statements

Feeling
statements

Intention
statements

Action
statements

GROUP OBSERVATION SHEET

As partners talk together in front of the group, use the spaces below to document your observation of the skills they use. Pick *one* skill to watch for and write it down in the space provided. Then write the names of the partners you will be observing. During their discussion, jot down words or phrases which document their use of the skill.

Skill: Skill:
Names:_____ _____   Names:_____ _____

Skill: Skill:
Names:_____ _____   Names:_____ _____

Skill: Skill:
Names:_____ _____   Names:_____ _____

AWARENESS OF OTHER

CHAPTER 2

TUNING IN TO YOUR PARTNER

Ask yourself:

How often do you really know what your partner thinks or feels?

How often are you sure that your partner understands what you are thinking and feeling?

How often do you discover that you and your partner have misunderstood each other?

How often has misunderstanding created difficulties for the two of you?

Suppose your answer to these questions runs something like this:

"There are times when one of us doesn't understand the other, and these misunderstandings have created difficulties. There are other times when I just wish my partner understood me better. And too often I am not sure I understand him/her either."

If your answer is anything like this, then it is very much like the ones given by most couples we know. Most of us would like to understand and be understood much more often than we are.

Understanding is an important ingredient in keeping relationships alive. When you and your partner understand one another, you increase your chances of working together well. Each of you has a good idea of what to expect from the other, and this creates a certain degree of predictability which makes it possible to trust. The sense of being understood that develops also increases our "connectedness" because this usually means we care enough about each other to try to understand.

Understanding does not occur automatically, even though the folklore of marriage suggests it should: "Couples who are really close know what each other thinks and feels and wants without a word being spoken." That isn't true, of course. And, as most of us know, good intentions are not enough, either. Instead, partners have to work hard to create understanding, and it takes communication skills too.

In the last chapter, we provided tools to help you disclose yourself more completely to your partner. This helps your partner understand you better. In this chapter, we will introduce tools to help you understand your partner better. Using these two sets of tools will help you and your partner reduce misunderstandings a great deal. Nevertheless, misunderstandings will occur. So, in addition, we will give you a procedure for clarifying misunderstandings as they arise.

ATTENTIVE LISTENING AND OBSERVING

The first rule for understanding your partner is this: Pay attention. Unless you pay careful attention to what your partner is saying and doing, you simply will not be able to understand him/her very well. It is easier said than done, however, because of our general listening habits.

Most of us have habits which keep us from paying full attention to the other person. Often we only pay partial attention because we are rehearsing our next speech instead. At other times, as we listen, we mainly evaluate what the other person is saying, forming judgments about whether it is right or wrong, good or bad, or whether we agree or disagree. Listening like this usually involves comparing our own viewpoint with the other person's. When we listen this way, we keep ourselves front and center, just as when we rehearse our next speech, and focus our attention more on our own experience than on the other person.

The habit of listening with only one ear is hard to break, and it can have significant impacts on your relationship with the other person. Even though it's tough to break bad habits, however, we can really listen— forget about our own speeches, suspend judgments, avoid comparisons— and just listen. Remember, full attention, careful listening, your total presence is a precious gift you can give to your partner. It's a gift that communicates care and concern.

Careful listening involves paying attention to *all* the sensory data coming to you. Your partner's facial expressions, body movement, posture, and breathing rate all convey messages, as well as the words s/he speaks and the tone, volume, and tempo s/he uses. Try to take in as much data as you can because what you sense becomes the basis for your interpretations.

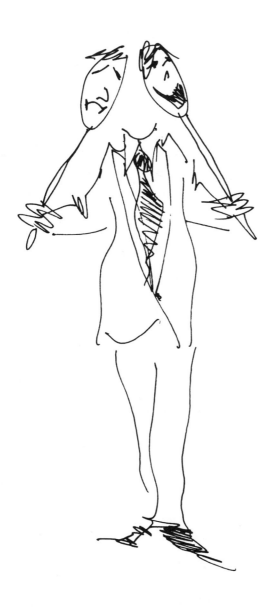

There are several aids to focusing your attention on your partner. Foremost of these is a tool now familiar to you: the Awareness Wheel. Try using the Awareness Wheel as you listen to boost your sensitivity to several different, important parts of each message. With the Awareness Wheel in hand you are prepared to:

— Listen for *sense* statements, "Jimmy came home from school crying today."

— Listen for *interpretation* statements, "I figured he had gotten hurt on the way home, but after he quieted down enough to talk, I realized his fingers and ears were freezing from the cold."

— Listen for *feeling* statements, "I felt so bad—really kinda guilty—about not insisting he wear his hat and mittens this morning!"

— Listen for *intention* statements, "I wouldn't want this to happen again."

— Listen for *action* statements, "From now on, I'm going to use my own judgment about how cold it is and whether he needs mittens."

Do not expect your partner to touch on every dimension of awareness when s/he speaks to you, any more than you would talk that way ordinarily. Often we use only one or two dimensions of the Awareness Wheel when we are talking about routine events. But you can notice which dimensions are talked about, and you can ask for other parts if you would like to know. To do this, often it is helpful to respond initially by using the same parts of awareness to let your partner know s/he is being heard. Then lead into other parts if you want more complete information:

Marlene: "I was feeling really good, almost kind of giddy, so I began singing out loud. As I walked by you, I said, 'Come on, sing along with me.' But you wouldn't, you just kept on reading. Then I felt kind of frustrated and a little stupid, too."

Hal: "I sort of remember seeing you hopping around and singing, feeling very carefree. What were you trying to do when you asked me to sing along?"

Two simple procedures will also help you listen more attentively and, at the same time, let the other person know s/he's being heard.

Echoing plays back your partner's exact words to let him/her know s/he's been heard. It is especially useful when s/he's giving you key information such as a telephone number, a time to meet, or dollar figures.

Ann: "Let's plan to meet at 5:30."

Jim: "At 5:30? Okay."

Paraphrasing plays back your partner's message in your own words rather than your partner's original words. In paraphrasing, you play back a piece of what you have just heard to let him/her know you are listening and encourage him/her to continue.

Mark: "We were just driving along, thinking of nothing in particular, not trying to do anything special..."

Ellen: "Just passing the time."

Mark: "Right. And then, when we got downtown..."

Echoing and paraphrasing help you to listen attentively, and they let your partner know you are listening. These procedures also can serve to help correct mistakes you might make in what you thought you heard, such as the wrong time or place.

Echoing and paraphrasing too much may annoy your partner, but if you have made little use of these before, you may have to overuse them for awhile just to get these skills well established. We recommend that you and your partner make agreements to tolerate the overuse of new skills, at least temporarily, so that you can become more comfortable using them.

ENCOURAGING/INVITING DISCLOSURE

The techniques we have talked about so far are designed mainly to help *you* listen more attentively and accurately. But there is a bonus, too: when you use them, your partner may find you easier to talk with because these skills help your partner to self-disclose. Now we would like to mention some other things you can do to make it easier or more pleasant for your partner to talk with you.

You can give a number of *nonverbal cues* which suggest you are interested and want him/her to continue: a nod of the head, a smile, eye contact, an "uh-huh" or "ummmm," and simple *verbal* acknowledgements such as "good," or "that's interesting." Another clear and simple way to indicate your interest is to put aside other things you are doing (the newspaper, sewing, the T.V.) and give your partner undivided attention. Think about it: don't you find it easier to talk with someone when they have put aside everything else and are paying attention only to you?

Sometimes you will find it useful to give more direct invitations:

"I'd like to hear more."

"Can you fill me in on what's happening?"

"Is there anything else you think would be useful for me to know?"

Now, a word of *caution* about use of these behaviors: Being too active—asking too many questions, paraphrasing back too quickly, or using too many nonverbal cues—may become disruptive and interfere with spontaneity. When and if this occurs, you will probably know it from your partner's response, and you can then change your pace.

CHECKING OUT

Attentive listening is necessary if you are going to understand your partner better, but sometimes it isn't enough. Your partner may not tell you everything you would like to know, or s/he may send a confusing message. Then it is time to become more active to increase the information you are receiving. You can do this by using the skill of checking out to ask your partner what is going on in his or her Awareness Wheel.

When you check out, you tune into your partner's Wheel by asking open questions about specific parts of the Wheel:

What do you think?

How do you feel?

Where do you want to go?

You can use these kinds of questions to check out any part of your partner's awareness when you want more complete information.

When you are confused about one of your partner's messages, you can use these kinds of questions to clarify your confusion. If, for example, your partner criticizes you ("you should be more considerate"), but you do not know what s/he is referring to, you can check out the basis of his/her interpretation by saying: "Hey, I'm not sure what you're talking about. What did I do that was inconsiderate?"

Checking out can also be used when you have made an interpretation and want to find out if it is accurate. You can check out these impressions or assumptions by letting your partner know what they are and asking whether they are correct:

"I know that you agreed to going out with the Morgans Saturday, but I have the impression you wanted to please me. You looked kind of disappointed when I suggested it. Are you?"

"Half the time during our conversation you've been laughing and joking, and several times you've changed the subject. This leads me to think you don't want to discuss the problem now. Is that true?"

In each example, the speaker made an interpretation about the partner's thoughts, actions, or intentions, then told how s/he arrived at the conclusion, and finished by asking whether the conclusion fit with the other's experience. This kind of check-out lets your partner know you have drawn a conclusion about him/her, but that it is only a tentative one and your partner has the final say on what s/he is experiencing. You gain information and at the same time show respect for your partner's integrity. It is often a nifty way to clear the air.

Like any other tool, checking out can be misused or abused. One common misuse of checking out is to ask questions simply as a way of disguising statements about yourself. For example:

disguised statement	*direct statement*
"Don't you think it would be better if we both went to talk with Jenny's teacher?"	"I want you to go with me to talk with him."
"Aren't you interested in Jenny's progress at school?"	"I'm angry and disappointed that you haven't agreed to go with me to the school."

These are *closed* or *leading questions* designed to persuade or somehow move the partner to agree. They are not intended to gain information.

Part of the skill of checking out is to avoid unnecessary use of why-questions. Stop reading for a moment and recall the last time someone

asked you a why-question. Do you recall feeling on the spot? This is a typical reaction to why-questions. You feel challenged, and called upon to justify yourself or defend a position.

When you find yourself about to ask a why-question, you can usually find a way to restate it as a what-, where-, how-, who-, or when-question. This will help you to get information instead of just a reaction. For example:

why-question	*open question*
"Why is Betty grounded?"	"What is Betty grounded for?"
"Why are you getting a new car instead of a used one?"	"What happened to change your mind about getting a used car rather than a new one?"

Sometimes, especially if the subject is a sensitive one, you can further reduce the sense of challenge by changing your why-question into a statement in which you self-disclose as well as check out:

"I'm really curious about how you happened to change your mind about getting a new car; because when we talked about it yesterday, I thought we agreed that a used one was a much better buy."

In this we are assuming the speaker is truly curious and not angry. If s/he is upset, more self-disclosure would be appropriate, particularly of feelings.

Another misuse of checking out is to use it to divert attention from yourself. You ask all sorts of open questions in order to keep the spotlight on the other person and off you. This kind of interviewing is frequently done when you have just met another person and want to learn something about him/her in a cautious way. But usually this type of caution is inappropriate when partners are talking. Often it creates an impression that you are trying to pry information from your partner while keeping your own cards close to your chest. That's not a very good way to build trust between you and your partner. Self-disclosing, along with checking out, will do more for building understanding and trust.

In short, checking out can be an extremely helpful communication tool, but all too often it is not even used. Instead, people simply rely on guesses as a basis for understanding their partners. When they guess right, everything is fine, but when they guess wrong, misunderstanding is the sure result. It is no wonder that learning to check out can have such a powerful impact on a relationship, as it did for a friend of ours who had participated in a Couple Communication group:

> "I discovered that when I don't know what my wife thinks or how she feels about something, I don't have to wait and wonder until she happens to tell me. I can *ask!* As simple as it is, I hadn't done this earlier in our marriage. When I learned to check out, it had a freeing-up effect for me in our relationship."

SHARED MEANING — TO INSURE ACCURACY

Did you ever find yourself in a situation where you and your partner agreed to something, only to learn later that what *you* agreed to was not what *your partner* agreed to? Or, did you ever get into an argument with someone, an argument which you carried on diligently and intelligently, only to finally discover that you were arguing about two quite different things? In each instance you were the victims of "unshared meanings."

When you stop to think about it, it is not surprising that unshared meanings happen. Communication is so complex! Even when we speak the same language, we each have our own special meanings for many things. Each person experiences in his/her own way. Each has a life history not duplicated exactly by any other, so between any two people, there is always the possibility for difference of meanings around the same event or same words.

Many of the misunderstandings you have experienced, many of the times you have been mis-heard or have mis-heard someone else, have resulted simply from the way language and life are. They have nothing to do with intelligence or good will, or sometimes even whether or not you were paying attention. Using the Awareness Wheel—the skills for self-disclosure and for tuning in to your partner—will help enormously in understanding and being understood. But these skills do not *guarantee* that you will understand your partner as s/he intended or that s/he will understand you as you intended in every instance. Sometimes you tell your partner something, and s/he adds on to the message a bit:

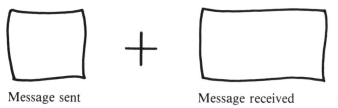

Message sent   Message received

At other times you tell your partner something, and his/her understanding of your message leaves out an important part:

Message sent   Message received

What we have just said about your messages applies equally to your partner's messages too. You may be "hearing" more or less than s/he intended.

When what you have told your partner is understood by her/him exactly as you intended, or vice versa, the two of you have a *shared meaning:*

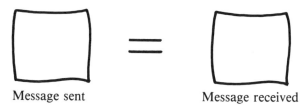

Message sent   Message received

A shared meaning occurs when the message sent by one person is the same as the message received by the other.

Much of the time it does not matter if there is a little slippage and the message sent is not *exactly* the same as the message received. *Approximately* will do well enough, and we need take no special action to assure that we have a shared meaning. Other times, message accuracy is quite important. Giving and receiving travel directions and agreements as to time and place of meeting are occasions when you want to be sure that you understand each other exactly. These are perhaps obvious.

Less immediately obvious, but even more crucial, are those occasions when you are discussing important issues, clarifying your positions, or making decisions. Many times the difficulties partners have in resolving an issue can be traced to one or more unshared meanings. Quite literally, they misunderstood one another. When the message is important and when it seems that it may be misunderstood, or has been misunderstood, you can use the *Shared Meaning Process* as an accuracy check.

The Shared Meaning Process begins when you or your partner *state an intention to share a meaning.* You may be referring to something your partner just said to you—a shared meaning about your partner's message. Or you may be referring to something you want to tell your partner—a shared meaning about your message.

Suppose you have told your partner you want to share a meaning about his/her message because you think you may not have understood it correctly. In the next step, you *report back in your own words* what you heard your partner telling you. Your partner then either *confirms* that your report was correct or *clarifies* the original message by resending the parts that were left out or misunderstood.,

When the shared meaning is about your message, you start it by stating your intention to share a meaning. The process continues with your partner *reporting back* to you his/her understanding of your message. Then you *confirm* his/her accuracy, or you *clarify* your initial message, if s/he was not accurate.

A Shared Meaning Process most often begins when one partner thinks s/he misunderstood something important that the second partner has said. Here is an example:

"I don't like it when your mother
comes to visit."

"Hey stop the train. I'd like   *stating intention*
to be sure I'm reading you right.   *to share meaning*
Okay?"

"Okay."

"What I understand you to mean is   *reporting back*
that you wish she wasn't coming.   *the message*
Is that it?"

"That's partly correct. I just feel   *clarifying the*
annoyed at the fact that she will   *original message*
be with us for two weeks. I'm
afraid I won't get much time with
you alone when she's here."

"The main thing is, we don't get   *reporting back*
enough time alone together when   *a second time*
she's here."

"Right. That's what I was really   *confirming*
getting at. Now, what would you
think about...."

Now this couple can go about planning how to make the visit less difficult.

Another couple, lacking knowledge of the Shared Meaning Process, might have covered the same subject this way:

"I don't like it when your mother comes to visit."

"Well, I can't tell her not to come!"

"I never said you should!"

This couple may never get around to planning how to make the visit more pleasant.

THE SHARED MEANING PROCESS

Let's look at the Shared Meaning Process in a little more detail. Typically, a shared meaning is begun during the course of an on-going conversation. An ordinary conversation typically involves statements and responses which build upon the same topic, with a shift in topic occurring periodically.

Ordinary Conversation

Person A   Person B

Statement

Response/Statement

Response/Statement

Response/Statement

When a Shared Meaning Process occurs in the midst of a conversation, it seems to stop the forward flow of conversation. Instead, the flow goes backward and around for a few moments.

Shared Meaning Process

Person A   Person B

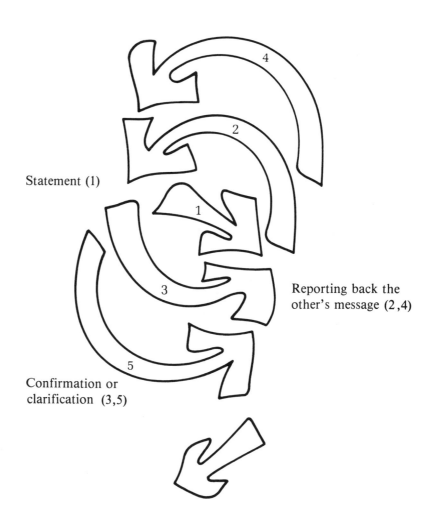

Statement (1)

Reporting back the
other's message (2,4)

Confirmation or
clarification (3,5)

The Shared Meaning Process can be completed quickly, in as few as three steps:

—Stating intention to share a meaning.

—Reporting back the message in your own words.

—Confirming the accuracy of the report.

More often, it takes more time and more steps as the sender clarifies the original message and the receiver reports back his/her understanding of the clarification. The process is not finished until message sent equals message received.

Who determines when message sent equals message received? The sender of the original message does. This is because only the sender really knows what s/he meant. Sometimes it's tempting for a receiver to stop the process by saying something like, "Okay, I've got it—I understand." Try to resist this temptation and see the process through to completion. And when you are a sender, make sure you confirm when message sent does equal message received.

Let's look at another example, this time illustrating a shared meaning started by the sender:

"I'd like to know what you are hearing me say because this is important to me. Okay?"	*stating intention to share meaning*
"Okay."	
"I'm feeling pulled two ways about taking that extra assignment. I want to do it because it's a challenge. But I don't think I want all the worries that would go with the job. I don't really know what to do."	*original message*
"What I'm hearing is you want two things that seem to be incompatible—to accept the challenge, which is likely to mean more worries, but also you want to avoid taking on more worries than you have right now. You're feeling uncertain how to resolve it."	*reporting back the message*
"That's it. That's where I'm at. It just seems like a big problem to me right now. What are your thoughts about it?"	*confirming (and moving forward with the conversation)*

We have now illustrated two ways to get a Shared Meaning Process started. First, a receiver states an intention to share a meaning, then reports back the other's message. Second, a sender states an intention to share a meaning and then sends a message.

Sometimes you may think your partner has said something important but find the message very confusing. Instead of trying to report back the message, simply ask your partner to restate the message. If you do not think you understand it the second time, you can start a shared meaning at that point. This might have been appropriate in the first illustration:

"I don't like it when your mother
comes to visit."

"Hey, wait a second. I didn't   *asking for*
understand what you mean.   *restatement*
Would you explain that again?"

"Sure. I just feel annoyed...."

Here is another tip about shared meaning. When your partner has delivered a long and complicated speech, trying to report back all of the message is nearly impossible. In this situation, ask him/her to slow down and take one part of the message at a time. What you are doing is creating a series of shared meanings to establish understanding of the total message.

What are the signs that a shared meaning has been achieved? If you were watching the process, you would often see both persons nod their heads, give some kind of facial recognition (often a smile) and move their bodies spontaneously, without hesitation. They are naturally signalling to each other that the Shared Meaning Process is complete. If there is any hesitation in facial expression or body movement, this usually signals that the meaning is only partially shared.

When two people achieve a shared meaning, both feel good about it even though they may have different points of view about the message. It gives both persons the confidence that understanding has occurred, and that the conversation can move forward from a point of understanding rather than from a point of misunderstanding.

Over years of teaching the Shared Meaning Process, we have noticed several interesting features about it:

—There is greater difficulty in achieving shared meaning when the message has emotional impact.

— There is greater difficulty when the statement is long and complicated.

— It is easier to achieve when the message contains all or most parts of the Awareness Wheel.

— For the one reporting back the message, there is a tendency to *reply* or talk *about* the message rather than report back the message.

— The sender of the message sometimes confirms too quickly, out of concern not to appear "picky."

Finally, the Shared Meaning Process has not only proven useful to thousands of couples but we have found that couples can quickly learn how to do it. It does take practice, so try to share a meaning with your partner once in awhile.

AGREEMENT/DISAGREEMENT

Paying careful attention, checking out, and sharing meaning when necessary will increase your understanding of your partner and his/her understanding of you. As this understanding develops, you will realize that you and your partner differ on many things. Sometimes you may find that you strongly disagree. There is a good reason for this: because both of you are unique, you are bound to differ in a number of ways. Out of these differences, disagreements are certain to arise.

Differences and disagreements between any two people are natural. Unfortunately, many people do not recognize this. Instead, they view disagreements as a sign that there is something wrong in the relationship: so they go to great lengths to maintain a facade of agreement.

The fear of differences and disagreements grows out of a more fundamental view of the nature of reality: There is a single, true reality. Either you or I have the true picture. If we disagree, one of us must be right and the other wrong. A natural consequence of taking this view is to see differences or disagreements as challenges to the truth, something which must be refuted and proved wrong.

Reality is more complicated than this, says another view. This view emphasizes that the picture each of us holds is only part of reality. Sharing our parts will help each of us understand more of the total picture. A natural consequence of taking this view is to see differences or disagreements as opportunities to learn.

When you and your partner meet your differentness or find yourself in disagreement, you can adopt the first point of view and take it as a threat. Or you can accept the second view and treat the situation as an opportunity to explore topics and issues, increase understanding of one another, and develop a more satisfying togetherness out of your appreciation of individuality. This is the climate that breeds true intimacy. These opportunities arise frequently if you look for them, even in ordinary, every-day events. Let's listen to a couple leaving a movie:

Liz: "I really enjoyed that."

Chuck: "You did? I didn't much like it. What did you like about it?"

Liz: "I liked all the little touches the director added, things that helped bring out the characters and make them come alive. I guess another thing I liked was the supporting actors. They were really outstanding."

Chuck: "What you liked about it was the technical details and the quality of acting. Is that right?"

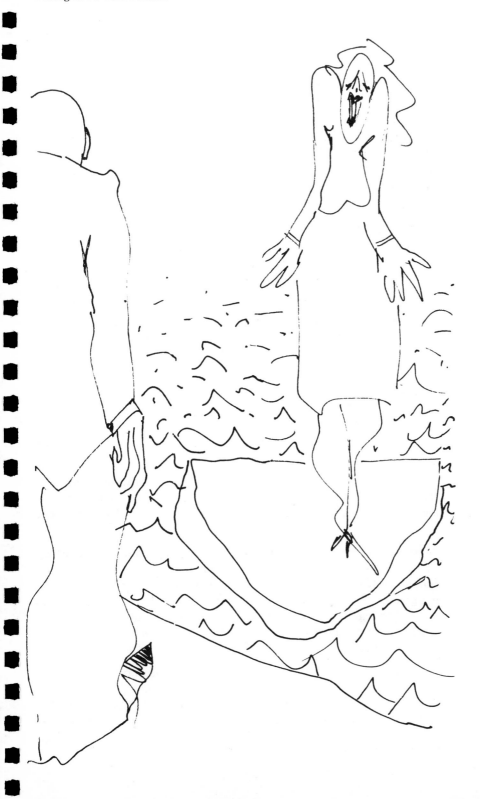

Liz: "Yeah."

Chuck: "I guess I'm mainly concerned with the action, the story. I
          have to lose myself in the story in order to enjoy it, and this
          movie didn't do that for me."

Chuck and Liz started with different evaluations of the movie, and they
ended with different evaluations. Each maintained the integrity of his
own experience of the movie; yet, at the same time, each gained an
understanding of what the other's experience of the movie was like.

Chuck and Liz shared their experiences with the aid of several of the
skills we have talked about so far:

Each *spoke for self,* and each managed to avoid speaking for the
other.

Chuck *checked out.* He invited disclosure from Liz without using
closed or leading questions. Liz responded with information as to
what she liked about the movie.

Chuck *paraphrased* Liz' statement to let her know that he heard her
and then provided information about what he likes in movies.

How might their conversation have gone if they viewed differentness
as a threat and lacked communication skills? Perhaps like this:

"That was a great movie!"

"How can you say that? It was lousy!"

"You're just being disagreeable. What's the matter with you
tonight?"

When a couple lacks appreciation for differences, they may push too
rapidly for agreement and fail to expand their understanding of one
another. Or sometimes they withdraw and then feel isolated from one
another.

With all this emphasis on the value of differences and disagreements,
you might be wondering if any agreement is necessary. Yes, it is. Two
people probably cannot live together with comfort and trust if they
disagree totally. On the other hand, most relationships can accept much
more difference and disagreement than is commonly thought. How
much you and your partner accept is likely to be an individual matter,
something that only the two of you can judge for yourselves.

We hope you will remember that when differences or disagreements
arise, there is a significant opportunity for personal and relationship
development. This development is much more likely to depend on
creating understanding between the two of you than on gaining agreement.

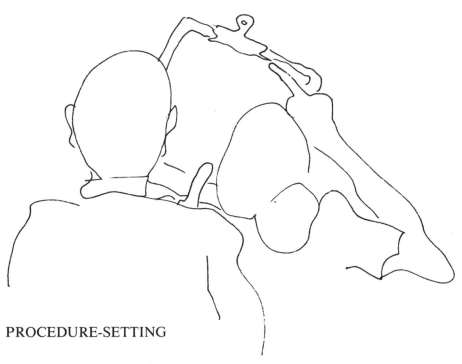

PROCEDURE-SETTING

One area where agreement is necessary is in the procedures you and your partner use when discussing issues. Nothing can undermine your discussion quicker than failing to agree on your procedures. For example, if one of you wants to talk about an issue but the other doesn't think it is the right time or place, the odds are pretty small that anything will be accomplished. That is when *procedure setting* can help you out.

Setting procedures simply means that you and your partner check out whether each of you wants to discuss the issue now or at some other time. You may also check to see whether the two of you agree concerning some other factors which can have a big impact on how well your discussion goes. These factors are listed below:

Factors in Procedure Setting

Issue	what
Procedures	whose
	who
	where
	when
	how
	energy
	length
	stopping

This is what we mean by each of these factors:

1.   *What* to talk about.

      This is the issue itself. Establishing agreement about what you want to talk about is a good starting point.

2.   *Whose* issue it is.

      Is it mine, yours, ours? This is particularly important to clarify when an issue is mine and does not involve you, but I want you to be a consultant to my concern.

3.   *Who* is included.

      Sometimes you will prefer to talk privately without children or other persons present. Other times you will want certain people included in the discussion.

4.   *Where* to talk.

      Place is important. There are some places conducive to good discussion, but other places can be distracting.

5.   *When* to talk.

      Timing is very important, especially if you are focusing on a sensitive or difficult issue. It is best to pick an occasion when you both feel ready to talk and you can give the time the issue deserves.

6.   *How* to talk.

      Shall we have an old-fashioned win/lose debate, or shall we attempt to figure out a solution together in which we both will realize our main objectives? Shall one of us act mainly as a facilitator to the other, for example, when the issue is one partner's only?

7.   *Energy* available for dealing with the issue.

      Some issues are best reserved for times when both of you have energy to handle them.

8.   *Length* of the discussion.

      You have probably had the experience of beginning a discussion and at 2:00 or 3:00 in the morning asking yourself, "Why didn't we just stop at midnight and plan to take it up later?" Sometimes it is a good idea to say ahead of time when you will stop, if the discussion has not been brought to closure.

9. *Stopping* the discussion.

    This factor is closely related to length of discussion. It is important that you have some common rule for stopping a discussion when one or both of you want to do so. Having an agreed upon way·to stop will allow you time to deal with issues and to postpone further discussion when you run out of steam.

We are not suggesting that you should run down this list *every* time you want to discuss an issue, whether it is big or small. Many couples have told us, however, that regularly checking out each other's willingness to talk before they begin has helped keep their discussions more focused and constructive. Occasionally it is very helpful to take more of these factors into account before you start talking.

When you and your partner can agree on procedures for handling issues, you have often done half the job. That's because the spirit of willingness to work together and support each other is a powerful force in a relationship. When it is present, you can use differences and disagreements for growing.

Using the skills from these two chapters can help you create understanding. Recognize, however, that misunderstanding can still occur, and when you think it is happening, take action. Pull out the Awareness Wheel at times like that and check it out. Use it to pay close attention to your partner's message. Use it to ask yourself and your partner what is meant, felt, or intended. Share a meaning. Or look at your procedures.

KEY IDEAS FROM CHAPTER 2

1. Maintaining awareness of your partner is just as important as maintaining self-awareness for effective communication.

2. There are several skills you use to maintain your awareness of your partner:

    —attentive observing and listening,
    —encouraging and inviting your partner to self-disclose,
    —checking out your partner's Awareness Wheel,
    —using the Shared Meaning Process when accuracy is important.

3. The Shared Meaning Process involves a minimum of three steps:

    —stating intention to share meaning,
    —reporting back the message in your own words,
    —confirming/clarifying.

4. Understanding and being understood is essential to maintaining a gratifying marital relationship.

5. Your differences and disagreements provide opportunities to grow.

6. Procedure-setting can help keep your discussions constructive.

AVOIDING MISUNDERSTANDING   Individual

Think back to recent discussions with your partner and try to identify *two* times when a Shared Meaning might have helped to avoid a misunderstanding. For each situation, answer these questions:

    a.   What was the topic of discussion?
    b.   What was the specific misunderstanding?
    c.   How did you feel following the misunderstanding?

	First situation	Second situation
a. topic		
b. misunderstanding		
c. your feelings		

Now try to list several cues or signals that would be useful for you and your partner to help you start a Shared Meaning when important misunderstandings crop up in the future.

LISTENING FOR FEELINGS

Individual

List five feelings/emotions you think your partner experiences frequently. For each emotion, give an example to document when you thought your partner was experiencing this emotion.

Emotion	Example
1.	
2.	
3.	
4.	
5.	

Share your list and examples with your partner if you wish and check out your accuracy with him/her.

PATTERNS OF CONVERSATIONS

Individual/Partner

Draw and divide the two boxes in the space below into four parts to indicate: (a) your own pattern in conversations with your partner; (b) your partner's pattern during conversations with you. Let the size of each part indicate the percentage of time you or your partner spend on each type of message: topic, self, partner, or relationship. These four types of messages were discussed in the Introduction. Example A indicates a pattern of equal attention to all four types. Example B indicates a pattern of heavy attention to topics and self.

Example A

topic	self
partner	relationship

Example B

topic	self
partner	relationship

Your pattern

Partner's pattern

After completing this exercise, compare your perceptions with your partner.

PROCEDURE SETTING

Individual/Partner

Think back to when you and your partner tried to deal with issues recently. Pick one successful time and one unsuccessful one, and answer these questions:

	Successful	Unsuccessful
a. What was the issue?		
b. Whose issue was it?		
c. Where did you talk?		
d. When did you talk?		
e. How long did you talk?		
f. How did you stop the discussion?		

Now compare the procedures you used in these two situations. Any similarities? Any differences? What factor(s) do you think made the difference between success and lack of success? Were the procedures you used in these two situations similar to the typical procedures you and your partner use when you deal with issues? If not, how do your typical procedures differ?

Next, share your perceptions with your partner and talk to him/her about the typical procedures you use.

DISCUSS AN ISSUE   Individual/Partner

Together with your partner, choose a current concern or issue in your relationship and talk about it, using the self-disclosure skills. Before discussing the issue, however, spend a few minutes organizing your awareness about the issue. Use the Awareness Wheel to do this.

Try to keep your discussion to about ten minutes.

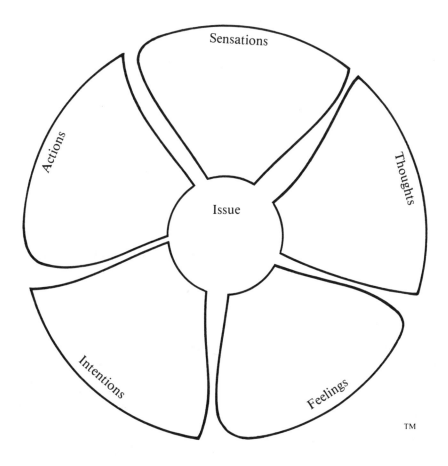

Tape Recording

This exercise is a good one to tape. After you have finished your ten-minute discussion, replay the tape and listen for your use of the skills. Be sure to focus on your *own* contribution to the discussion—your use of skills—not on your partner's. You may want to use a Tape Observation Sheet to keep track of your use of the skills.

TUNING INTO YOUR PARTNER'S PERSPECTIVE   Partner

Choose two topics from those listed below and check out your partner's views. Be sure to ask about the different parts of his/her Awareness Wheel—what s/he thinks, feels, wants, etc., regarding the topic.

This exercise is designed to help you tune into your partner's self-awareness and to practice listening. If you think you may not have understood him/her correctly, feed back what you have heard to see whether you have understood his/her point of view.

After your partner has given a picture of his/her awareness, share your perspective. If differences between the two of you occur, try not to become persuasive. Rather, see if you can allow and appreciate these differences. Spend no more than five minutes per topic.

Topics

relating to your children   personal goals

how you see me trying to control you   things you enjoy about me

handling or saving money   how you see my commitment to you

a spiritual experience   ways we compete with each other

friends of the opposite sex

CHECKING OUT YOUR PARTNER'S AWARENESS   Partner

At different times during the week, check out with your partner what s/he is thinking, feeling, wanting, etc., at that specific point in time.

SHARED MEANING EXERCISE   Partner

This exercise provides practice using the Shared Meaning Process and all the skills you have learned so far. Exchange *two* shared meanings with your partner concerning something positive about (a) yourself, and (b) you in relation to your partner.

One partner be sender and the other receiver. First, one partner sends a positive message about him/herself, keeping these things in mind:

—Be certain of the meaning you intend.

—Remember what you mean and how you say it.

—Make a brief statement—one or two sentences—including several dimensions of your Awareness Wheel.

—Try to send the message clearly and directly; this exercise is designed to share a meaning with your partner, not confuse him/her.

Receiver reports back sender's message, keeping these things in mind:

—Restate in your own words all the meanings you receive.

—Do not respond to the sender's statement.

—Do not guess at your partner's meaning (e.g., "Do you mean...?" "You mean...," or "I think you mean..."). If you don't understand, simply tell your partner you don't and ask him/her to send the same message again.

The sending partner then confirms the receiver's accuracy or clarifies his/her original message, being careful not to add to it. Continue reporting back and clarifying until sender confirms accuracy.

Switch roles with sender becoming receiver, and vice versa, and continue exercise until each partner has shared two messages.

Tape Recording

This exercise is a good one to tape. Listen for the use of the shared-meaning skills (particularly reporting back and confirming) and the self-disclosure skills. You may want to use a Tape Observation Sheet to help you listen for skills. Pay particular attention to your own contribution to the discussion rather than your partner's.

OLD OR NEW ISSUE   Group

1. Without consulting your partner, pick an issue you would like to discuss in front of the group with feedback from other group members and the instructor on your use of skills.

    a. What is the issue?

2. Now, sit with your partner, compare issues and decide:

    a. Whose issue you are interested in discussing?

        yours   mine   ours   (circle one)

    b. Whether or not you want to discuss the issue while group members listen?

        yes   no   (circle one)

3. If you are going to practice an issue in group with skill feedback, take a few minutes to reflect on your awareness of the issue. Jot down some key words and phrases in the Awareness Wheel.

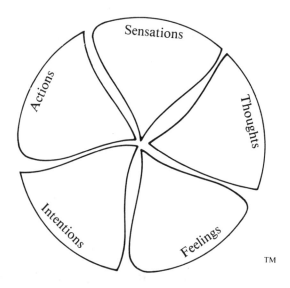

4. When your turn comes to discuss the issue with your partner, try to share complete and congruent awareness about the issue. Be careful not to make a long speech about your awareness—just exchange it with your partner. In the time available you will probably not be able to resolve the issue, but both of you will be able to share a good deal of your awareness.

PROGRESS REVIEW

Here's a chance for you to again review your progress in learning the skills, frameworks, and processes presented in the first two chapters. Rate yourself on each skill, process, and framework by placing an X in the appropriate box.

	Initial Learning	Awkward Use	Conscious Application	Natural Use
SKILLS				
Speaking for self				
Making sense statements				
Making interpretive statements				
Making feeling statements				
Making intention statements				
Making action statements				
Attentive listening and observing				
Encouraging/inviting disclosure				
Checking out				
PROCESSES				
Documenting interpretations with data				
Shared meaning process				
Setting procedures				
FRAMEWORKS				
Awareness Wheel				
Focus of Conversation				

TAPE OBSERVATION SHEET

As you listen to tapes from exercises in this chapter, jot down words or phrases that indicate your use of the various communication skills and behaviors.

Tape 1	Tape 2
Speaking for self	
Speaking for others	
Echoing/paraphrasing	
Encouraging/inviting disclosure	
Checking out	
Stating intention to share meaning	
Reporting back sender's message	
Confirming/clarifying	

GROUP OBSERVATION SHEET

Group

As partners talk together in front of the group, use the spaces below to document your observation of the skills they use. Pick *one* skill to watch for and write it down in the space provided. Then write the names of the partners you will be observing. During their discussion, jot down words or phrases which document their use of the skill.

Skill:
Names:_____ _____

Skill:
Names:_____ _____

Skill:
Names:_____ _____

Skill:
Names:_____ _____

Skill:
Names:_____ _____

Skill:
Names:_____ _____

STYLES OF COMMUNICATION

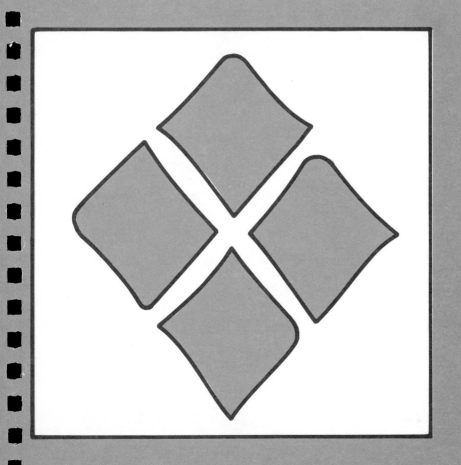

CHAPTER 3

FOUR WAYS OF TALKING

Have any of these things happened to you?

—You wanted to have a pleasant, sociable time but found yourself hassling your partner and being grouchy.

—You wanted to take charge but came off as if you were putting people down by bossing them around.

—You wanted to talk about some strong feelings you have had recently but found yourself skirting them with intellectual conversation.

Each time, how you talked—your style—just didn't match your intentions. The result was that you failed to get your point across, or you did not relate to your partner the way you wanted. This happens when your intention and communication style do not match.

In this chapter we will describe four styles of communication, four very different ways of talking. As you become familiar with them, you'll be better able to move flexibly from one style to another, matching the style with your intentions for each situation.

Flexibility is the key. Effective communicators are flexible. If you and your partner have all four styles at your command, you are prepared for any kind of talk together: to joke, debate, theorize, or relate intimately. Each of the four styles has its own important uses.

We will give most of our attention to Style IV, however, because this style requires the most effort to learn well. Also it is the style you are least likely to have learned when you were growing up. As a way of comparing the four styles let's listen in as four husbands talk to their wives about entertaining guests that night.

Style I.   "When I ate out with Bill last month, he told me that they really missed the seafood they used to have before they moved here. I hope the shrimp and scallops dish will be a big hit tonight.''

Style II.   ''Make sure you get the meal out on time. Last time you embarrassed me by not serving until 9:30. People expect to eat at a reasonable time, you know.''

Style III.   ''When we have guests we seem to crab at each other. I'm wondering if it's because we're so concerned about making everything just right that we forget about having fun.''

Style IV.   ''I'm excited about tonight but afraid we'll be at each other as usual during the last minute scramble before the guests come. I'd like to figure out a way to avoid a hassle.''

In each situation, the husband uses a different style. The differences in style result from differences in their intentions and in their behavior. Let's review:

—Husband #1 wants to keep their interaction on a sociable level *(intention)* so he chit chats *(behavior)*.

—Husband #2 wants to make sure something is done in a certain way *(intention)* so he issues orders and put downs *(behavior)*.

—Husband #3 wants to raise an issue very cautiously *(intention)* so he poses the issue tentatively and speculates about a possible reason *(behavior)*.

—Husband #4 wants to insure a good evening together with friends *(intention)* so he reports his feelings and makes an intention statement *(behavior)*.

To help you become more familiar with the four styles we are going to talk about each of them separately, how they connect with your intentions, and what behaviors go along with each style.

STYLE I

This friendly, conventional, and sometimes playful style keeps the world going. When you want to keep things moving in an easy and light way, you are likely to talk in Style I, on a level of sociability. This is why we refer to this as a sociable style.

Style I communication is essential to carrying on most ordinary activities. In this style, information is exchanged in a way that meets social expectations. Usually, the speaker's intentions are to be pleasant and courteous and not to change anything. There is a wish to communicate in a comfortable way.

Style I communication is characterized by the absence of any weighty issues and a lack of tension. The focus is on everyday topics and routine matters. Both you and your partner are content with the "space" you two are in together: no tug or push by either of you to move to anything serious. There is relatively little self-disclosure, and that feels comfortable to each of you at this time.

Many Style I statements suggest positive pairing between the two people involved. Often you and your partner indirectly demonstrate the basic fondness and attraction you feel for one another as you catch each other up on the events of your day, chit chat about people you know, or pass on a good story you heard at work. You are showing evidence of your mutual affection and enjoyment of each other without saying directly, "I like you. I have fun with you."

You most often use Style I in situations calling for:

—simple planning; "I'd like to stop at the supermarket on the way back."

—exchange of factual information; "The car stalls every time it rains. Probably needs a tune-up."

—keeping informed; "How did things go yesterday?"

—just being together; "You'd never guess what Timmy said today. He and Lucy were playing in the sandbox...."

Several dimensions of the Awareness Wheel may be involved in Style I messages. For example, sensations may be described, or thoughts and preferences shared. And action statements often occur in the telling of anecdotes or reporting of events. But direct disclosure of immediate and intimate feelings and intentions is missing.

You use Style I when your intentions are to keep the conversation on a sociable level:

conventional
friendly
playful
every day
routine

Style I behaviors are easily recognized. They consist of:

—reporting events and factual information; "The office closed at noon today."

—simple descriptions; "You're missing a button."

—routine questions; "Taste good?"

—joking and story telling; "I heard a good one today. It seems that..."

—low-key, unelaborated statements about such things as simple preferences; "I'd rather have tea, thanks."

—opinions and ideas; "I like contemporary furniture best."

—physical states; "I'm tired."

—actions; "I wrote to Jim yesterday."

Unlike several other styles, Style I has no highly distinct language characteristics. Furthermore, the vocal characteristics of Style I are normal so the tone of conversation is generally friendly, relaxed, and tension-free.

Style I is a comfortable place to be when you have no strong urge to change things or make something happen. But when you do have these urges, Style I is not a good match for your intentions. A better match is Style II.

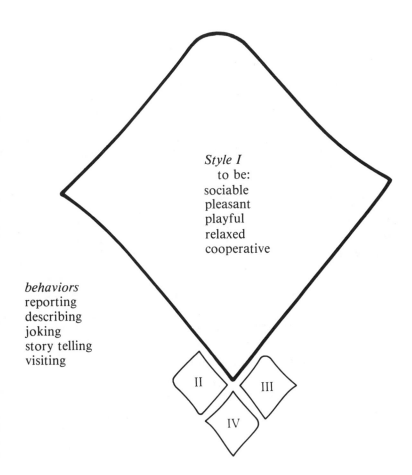

Style I
  to be:
sociable
pleasant
playful
relaxed
cooperative

behaviors
reporting
describing
joking
story telling
visiting

II

III

IV

STYLE II

Style II asserts your right to be in charge. This is why we call it a control style. You use Style II when you are shooting for a certain outcome and want things to happen in a certain way. Your goal may be to create change and make something happen. Or it may be to resist change and keep something from happening.

Generally Style II focuses on other persons, not on yourself, and you share little of your self-awareness. Your objective is to get the other person to agree or to do what you want so you usually do not give him/her much background information. With this focus, Style II can be brief and efficient, so it is no wonder that most of us use it quite often.

Style II, however, can backfire. In its brevity and efficiency, it can create misunderstanding, distance, and tension. This can happen even in situations where Style II is ordinarily quite appropriate.

As an example, let's consider this Style II statement: "Watch Tim while I finish cutting the grass." Sounds like a routine statement about dividing responsibilities, right? But not if this couple is stuck with an unresolved issue about sharing responsibility for child care. Then, this otherwise innocent directive may really set off something:

> "Don't tell me what to do! You're supposed to be watching Tim now, and you're not going to lay that on me. Do the lawn on your own time, not mine."

Actually, there are two kinds of Style II, as this example illustrates. The first statement was what we call Light Control Style. It is the kind of Style II you hear in everyday life in relatively tension-free settings when people are giving orders, instructing, advising, and selling. It is used to gain compliance or agreement through persuasive means.

The second statement was what we call Heavy Control Style. It is the Style II you hear when tension is high and feelings are strong. Then people are likely to pull out all stops to force change or to resist a demand for change. We will look at the two types of Style II separately.

LIGHT STYLE II

In everyday conversations, Light Style II is very common. You most often use it in situations calling for:

—legitimate authority as with a subordinate or a child; "No candy, Benny, We're having supper in just a few minutes."

—establishing expectations; "Church starts at 9:30, and we're all going together."

—dividing everyday responsibilities; "Scrub the kitchen while I vacuum the living room."

—messages signalling tension or dissatisfaction; "Next time you're going to be that late getting home, give me a call."

—encouraging approved behavior; "The car looks great. You did a good job waxing it."

—asserting your expertise; "Here, let me show you. It works best like this..."

—ventilating, letting off steam; "Boy, did I have a lousy day!"

Light Style II uses only part of your Awareness Wheel. Most statements involve interpretations, but sensations are seldom shared. Practically all involve intentions, too. More often than not, however, your intentions are implied by the form of the statement rather than stated directly. When Light Style II is used, feelings are not very strong so they are usually left out.

The intentions that form the basis for Light Control Style include:

persuasion
seeking agreement
exercising legitimate authority

Typical behaviors involved when you use Light Style II are:

—directing; "Take the car in for a tune-up."

—advising; "It would be better if you checked with John first before making plans."

—instructing; "See how this is done. First you..."

—persuading; "Come on, let's try it just once."

—selling; "Don't you think we should get the smaller one so we can save money?"

—praising; "Your painting is terrific."

Light Control Style frequently uses certain standard forms of statements—imperatives, closed questions, speaking for other. Vocal characteristics of Light Style II are relatively normal, though perhaps a bit loud, firm, and authoritative-sounding.

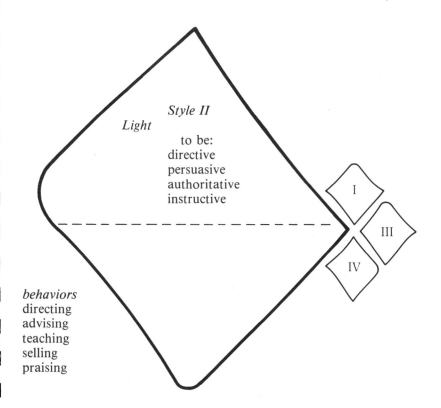

Style II

Light

to be:
directive
persuasive
authoritative
instructive

I

III

IV

behaviors
directing
advising
teaching
selling
praising

HEAVY STYLE II

Heavy Style II is most often used in situations involving considerable tension and strong feelings. It can be very active or very passive, but in both forms it is aggressive and the basic goals are the same: to force change or to resist attempts at change. You are into Heavy Control Style if you try to force agreement or force an outcome without regard for your partner's feelings or what your partner thinks or wants.

Another thing both active and passive forms of Heavy Style II have in common is that they are hazardous to self-esteem, your own as well as your partner's. Instead of focusing on a person's behavior or on an issue, Heavy Style II concentrates on the person himself, questioning or even attacking his/her motives and competence. Consequently, use of Heavy Style II can result in an explosion posing a threat to your relationship.

Sometimes such an explosion may serve a useful purpose as a signal that you are into a sensitive area which merits greater attention. However, you will not make much progress in your discussion until you have moved away from Heavy Style II.

When you are in an argument or a fight, Heavy Style II is likely to be the way you attack the other person and defend yourself. This style also crops up when you are in a power struggle with someone else. Heavy Style II usually comes to the fore as a reaction to tension or anger developing in a situation. Especially in its active form, this style literally explodes in the middle of a situation.

As with Light Style II, Heavy Style II leaves out most of your own Awareness Wheel, even though strong feelings and intentions usually are present when it is used. Instead, the feelings and intentions are *acted out* through a variety of nonverbal means—tone of voice, loudness, rate of speech, gestures, and various other actions. More than the other styles, this one operates from the adage, "actions speak louder than words," and avoids direct disclosure of most parts of the Awareness Wheel.

The intentions of Heavy Style II are to bring about change or resist it. But instead of the persuasive touch characteristic of Light Style II, as the tension and pressure develop in a situation, these intentions shift and become heavy handed—an intent to force change or to fight against attempts at change. In addition, other intentions may develop as well:

> hurting the other person
> making the other person feel guilty
> winning
> protecting and defending yourself
> avoiding responsibility

Heavy Style II uses a variety of tactics to achieve its ends. Some of the active behaviors are:

> —labelling; "That's just irresponsible."

> —name-calling; "You're just a weakling."

> —mind-reading; "You don't really believe that."

> —blaming; "This wouldn't happen if you weren't always late."

> —accusing; "Your eyes never left him for one moment!"

> —threatening; "This is your last chance."

> —demanding change; "You shouldn't feel that way."

> —evaluating; "You're wrong again."

> —put-downs; "Only a woman would do that."

> —ordering; "Stop it right now!"

Passive behaviors used as tactics in Heavy Style II include the following:

> —complaining; "I do all the dirty work around here and never get any help."

> —self-protecting; "That's not what I said."

> —disqualifying; "I didn't mean it that way."

> —withholding; "I told you once already. I'm not going to repeat it."

> —poor me; "I wish things would go my way just once."

> —pseudo-questions; "Will you tell me what's so terrible about having a little fun?"

> —foot dragging; "I'll get to it when I have time."

> —assuming blame; "You're right; it's all my fault."

—being a martyr; "It doesn't matter; I can take it. I always do."

—acting self-righteous; "Who are you to accuse me of something like that!"

Additionally, passive forms of Heavy Style II include keeping score, not answering your partner's questions, changing the topic, and silence—the quiet, angry type. All of these are powerful tactics for indirectly expressing sentiment and manipulating your partner.

Heavy Style II uses a variety of highly distinctive words: should, ought, have to, always, never, every, right, wrong, good, bad. It also uses the types of statements noted before for Light Control Style: imperatives, closed questions, speaking for other. Heavy Control Style is perhaps most easily recognized by its voice and speech characteristics: harsh, emotionally-charged, threatening or sarcastic tone, loud and negative sounding or soft and whiny, rapid rate.

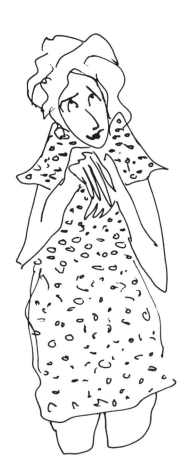

Most people grow up with a lot of exposure to Style II, both Light Control Style and Heavy Control Style; so, if you and your partner rely initially on Style II in attempting to deal with serious personal and relationship issues, that is only natural. Even with a sensitive issue, Style II may serve to help the issue to surface and be recognized as needing attention, and it may serve to let off a little emotional steam.

Style II is a dangerous style, though. The danger is not simply in using Style II; that's normal. The big danger is that after you and your partner try to deal with significant issues in Style II and find that you cannot, you give up trying and fail to deal with issues at all. This may happen because you do not want to quarrel and hurt each other. Sometimes it happens because partners have only limited communication skills and cannot move beyond Style II. This does not have to be the case, however. Other communication styles are available for effectively dealing with serious issues, and these styles can be learned. We will talk about them next.

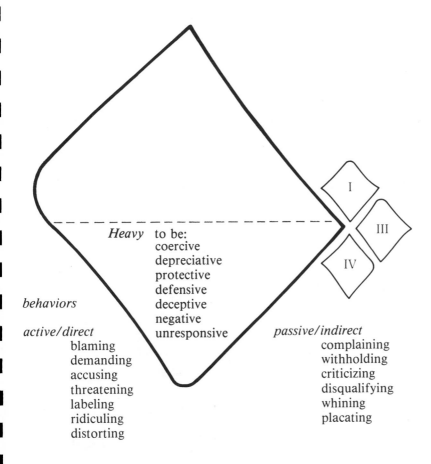

Heavy to be:
coercive
depreciative
protective
defensive
deceptive
negative
unresponsive

behaviors

active/direct
blaming
demanding
accusing
threatening
labeling
ridiculing
distorting

passive/indirect
complaining
withholding
criticizing
disqualifying
whining
placating

STYLE III

Style III is a tentative and speculative style in which you reflect on a situation or issue. Your orientation in Style III is quite different from that in Styles I and II. Rather than trying to keep things smooth, or to change and control, in Style III you sort of stop your world, reflect on it, and explore it. You examine an issue or event to determine what is behind it, or where it is going, and what you might best do about it. That's why we call Style III a searching style.

When Style III is used, there is almost always an issue present. Style III expresses interest in dealing with an issue intellectually but there is little emotion expressed nor commitment made to take action. The usefulness of the style lies in opening up ideas about the issue and expanding your options for the future.

Style III is most often used in dealing with non-routine situations, *i.e.,* when changes are occurring and you are uncertain about what directions to go:

"What about when the baby comes. Are we going to split the work equally, or would it be more practical for one of us to be the main 'mom' and the other to help out?"

Style III can help you identify and clarify issues you and your partner want to talk about:

"I don't think we've been having much fun together lately. What do you think?"

"Now that you mention it, I think that's probably right. Especially just you and I together, without the children."

"Maybe that's something worth exploring a bit."

Style III is useful for examining background information relevant to the issue:

(continuing conversation above) "Maybe it's because we don't have sitters handy any more since we moved here."

"Maybe so. We always had built-in sitters back in Dayton, with our parents nearby, and lots of friends to swap sitting with."

"Yeah, we never had to search out sitters before. It's like we just sort of drifted into a pattern of not going out except with the kids along."

Finally, Style III is useful in generating alternative courses of action:

"Maybe we could find another couple with young kids who don't have their folks living right near and who'd be interested in swapping sitting."

"Yeah, we may be able to find one through the couples club in church."

"Sounds good. I could check with the high school, too, to see if there's an organized sitter service. Or locate a kid in the neighborhood. Sometimes I'd just as soon pay somebody to sit and not have to figure out who owes whom a turn."

In Style III the interpretation dimension of the Awareness Wheel is used heavily. Action statements also are used quite a bit, but these tend to be descriptions of past behaviors, or tentative proposals for future actions. Style III sometimes uses sense statements to document interpretations, but it includes practically no feeling or intention statements.

Style III uses the skill of speaking for self with lots of statements beginning with "I," but most of these are "I think." Style III also makes liberal use of the skill of checking out. In Style III you are usually discussing past events or possible future events, so there is little focus on "what's happening right now" and no commitment to take action.

When you use Style III, your intentions are to be:

tentative
reflective
speculative
explorative

These intentions are expressed in Style III with behaviors such as these:

—use of open questions to check out; "How do you see it?"

—giving impressions; "It seems to me you've been working hard lately."

—paraphrasing; "It sounds like you feel more disappointed than angry."

—giving explanations; "I sometimes do that when I'm uncertain about something."

—speculating about causes; "Probably our marriage works so well because we have many of the same values."

—analyzing; "I think our arguments about money might possibly be related to a bigger issue."

—proposing alternative solutions; "Maybe we should lay down the law to the kids about this?"

—procedural comments; "Could we set aside some time to talk about our budget?"

The most distinctive language characteristic of Style III is the heavy use of qualifiers: probably, possibly, maybe, sometimes, perhaps, could, might. Otherwise, the vocal characteristics of Style III are pretty normal so that Style III sounds much like Style I.

To summarize briefly, Style III is useful when you are dealing with serious and sensitive issues. You can use it to identify the issue, explore relevant background information, and propose possible actions. However, because feelings, intentions, and future actions are expressed only tentatively—or not at all—Style III is a limited style. It does not move to the core of issues. To do this, you will need an additional style: Style IV.

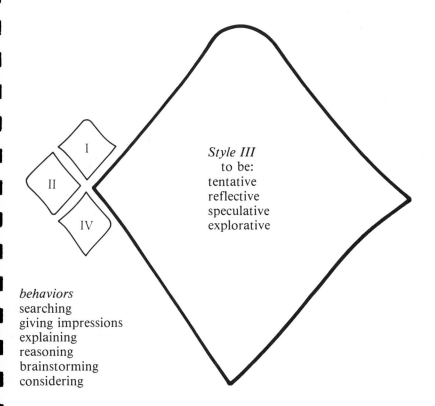

Style III
to be:
tentative
reflective
speculative
explorative

behaviors
searching
giving impressions
explaining
reasoning
brainstorming
considering

STYLE IV

When you and your partner deal with an issue in Style IV your communication is direct and action oriented. What you say goes to the core of the issue and deals with differences and tensions directly without blaming, demanding, or defending. You are interested in the present, rather than the past or future: what thoughts, feelings, intentions exist *now;* what choices are possible; which option you will put into action. Your attention is centered on your immediate experience—your Awareness Wheel—which you disclose completely and congruently. This is why we refer to Style IV as a centered style.

Style IV is characterized by three processes:

—You *acknowledge* your experience. This is done by tuning into your complete Awareness Wheel.

—You *accept* what you find. Sometimes this is difficult to do because your experience is painful, embarrassing or frightening. When this occurs you might find yourself denying your awareness by saying to yourself:

> I don't really feel that way, or
>
> I didn't mean that, or
>
> I don't really want that.

Failure to accept your complete awareness denies the validity of your experience. You short circuit your potential for understanding yourself more fully and acting in accordance with your full experience. Accepting your awareness prevents saying one thing and doing another.

—You *act* on your awareness. By using complete self-information you make more effective and satisfying decisions. Often your action includes openly sharing your awareness with your partner or someone else. Other times you may not involve others but act appropriately on your awareness without talking to anyone about it. Of course not all awareness demands action—sometimes you act by deciding not to act.

An essential part of Style IV is that it expresses your intention to value both yourself and your partner. In some ways this is the most important feature of Style IV because it captures the spirit of caring and mutual support. Personal and relationship growth cannot occur if the valuing of one partner and the building of his/her esteem occurs at the expense of the other. Putting yourself down or putting your partner down would undermine relationship development.

There is something paradoxical about Style IV. It is a good style to use in working toward a solution to a sensitive issue, but as soon as you try to use Style IV behaviors to win, you lose. It doesn't work. It becomes mechanical. The intention to have your own way is quite contrary to the cooperative spirit of Style IV communication. As soon as you try to use Style IV to force change, you move out of it.

Style IV is used most often to discuss non-routine situations which may crop up in several different ways:

—when a feeling of dissatisfaction develops for one of both partners: "I don't know how you're feeling, but I've been feeling down since last night; and it seems to me that I usually feel that way after an argument. I'd like to be able to get beyond feeling angry with you, then go on to other things, feeling okay."

—when circumstances change; "I heard something at the office today that I don't think you'll like to hear. The company is moving the whole regional staff to St. Louis. I'm really frustrated because I don't see any options. I would like to stay here and not move, but unless I leave the company or take a demotion, I think we'll have to move."

—when expectations are broken; "I'm really upset because a lot of the jobs haven't gotten done around here that we agreed to do. Like washing the windows. I have taken the curtains down three times in preparation for washing the windows."

—when you and your partner anticipate the future; "I've been feeling excited recently thinking about your going back to school. I'm not sure how we'll work it out financially, but I think it's important since it's something you've been talking about doing for a long time."

But Style IV is not limited to dealing with major issues. It's the style you use in other important situations as well:

—when you want to share something about an experience beyond simply reporting events of the day; "I learned something interesting about myself today. I was feeling dragged out and didn't want to be at work. I packed up a couple of times and then unpacked. Then I started to walk out the door, but there was somebody coming up the stairs so I snuck back into the room. I was feeling really silly about myself. Then I thought to myself, 'this is ridiculous, just leave!' So I told my boss I was going to leave, and she was immediately understanding—I wasn't aware before of how hard it is for me to leave my job, even when I've been working a lot of overtime recently."

—when you affirm your partner; "Jack, this morning I was thinking about how much I love you and how much I can count on you. A lot of women don't have the confidence I do because they don't have someone they can count on backing them up. Thanks—I really love you."

You really are intimate with your partner when you share your private world, your inner experience of feelings, desires and sensations.

Style IV uses all of your Awareness Wheel—your sensations, thoughts, feelings, intentions, and actions. It expresses all of these dimensions directly and openly, *acting on* your awareness instead of acting it out. Style IV tunes into all of your partner's Awareness Wheel, too. In effect, in Style IV you get all of your own information and all of your partner's information out on the table so all of it can be used. This helps the two of you use your different experiences to find better solutions. And in the process, both of you learn more about each other.

Style IV is a good style for you if your intentions are to be:

focused	responsive
direct	honest
clear	caring
responsible	collaborative

These are the kinds of intentions that serve as a basis for building intimacy with your partner.

Style IV talking uses all of the communication skills we have discussed so far. You speak for self to share all parts of your Awareness Wheel with your partner. You listen attentively and check out his/her Wheel, too. When there is a question of understanding a message accurately, you use the Shared Meaning process.

That's what Style IV is made of—these intentions and these skills and one thing more: a spirit of sharing and valuing both yourself and your partner. Listen as John and Karen, a couple in their mid-thirties, focus on a situation in their life.

John: "I get annoyed—it's more than that—upset with you when I don't hear appreciation from you for what I've done. Rather I hear kind of a discounting of it. The result of that is a real stubborn feeling on my part, that I'm not going to do anything now."

Karen: "Uh-huh. Can you give me an example?"

John: "Okay. The other morning when I'd gotten up with the kids and you were still in bed. I took care of the kids, got their breakfast, and got them dressed. When you got up to go somewhere that morning—I didn't have to go anywhere—I went back in and collapsed on the bed. I wasn't going back to bed or going back to sleep, but I was just laying there. You appeared to be very upset; I don't remember what you said, but I got a very clear message that you were upset with me for being so lazy as to go back to bed like that."

Karen: "As I remember that morning, I was folding clothes on the bed. This gets to the meat of the situation. While I stood there and folded clothes, you didn't help. That's what bugs me the most—when I'm doing something, like running around the house working on things, I see you watching TV, or even doing things that I think are worthwhile like reading, but it still bugs me. Part of that comes from the fact—I think it's a fact—that when you're busy doing something, I can't stop myself from helping you. I just wouldn't feel right about sitting watching TV while you folded the clothes. I'm getting (laughter) a look like maybe you don't believe that..."

John: "No, not at all, on the contrary. I've noticed that when I'm in doing the dishes, you come in there and kind of busy yourself in the kitchen."

Karen: "Yes, I do that."

John: "But I feel uncomfortable with that. I would prefer to have you reading a book or doing whatever you want. While I'm doing the dishes, I kind of have the idea that you're watching over my shoulder. Or it's more like the feeling is that my effort doesn't count for as much because you're working too."

Karen: "It's not my intention to make you feel ill at ease or like I'm looking over your shoulder or checking up on the kind of job you do. It's more my intention to let you know that I want to help, and also that I enjoy doing things together. I think that's why I discount to a certain extent some of the things that you do. Because often when I'm really busy working, you're not working, and that stays in my memory. If I was right there and you were working, I'd be helping you."

John: "So my work doesn't count for so much."

Karen: "Yeah, that's what I usually think. I want to add that it's not a big part of my thoughts about you, though. I heard you too. I'll try to recognize that you think differently than I do about helping out."

John: "And I'll try to remember that when you do help out, it's probably cause you want to be with me. You know I like that, too, when we're working together and accomplishing something. Let's both try to be more sensitive to each other, okay?"

Karen: "Okay."

You can identify Style IV by listening for the different parts of the Awareness Wheel. If you hear most parts being expressed, as in John and Karen's discussion, Style IV is being used. Style IV is usually delivered with a fairly normal tone and pitch, but the pace is often slower than other styles.

If you get the impression that we are excited about Style IV, you're right. We think it is a key that can open a door to a whole new world of experience for you and your partner. But we don't think it's best in every circumstance. It's too heavy for ordinary conversations and it's inefficient for handling everyday decisions. And you should think twice about using it with someone you do not trust: you become vulnerable when you disclose things to someone who might use them against you.

Even with your partner or with other people you trust, Style IV may feel risky. Yet nothing compares when partners want to deal with a sensitive issue, or when you just want to share yourself with your partner.

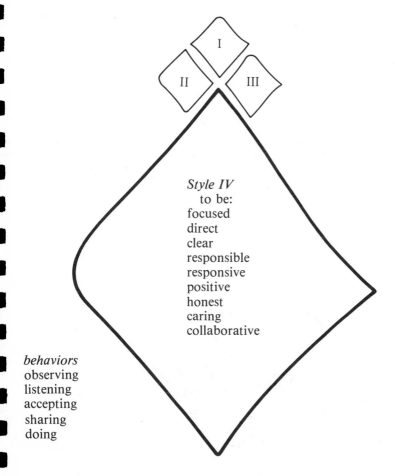

I

II   III

Style IV
    to be:
focused
direct
clear
responsible
responsive
positive
honest
caring
collaborative

behaviors
observing
listening
accepting
sharing
doing

SUMMARY OF STYLES

The four styles are most easily distinguished from one another in terms of intentions and behaviors. You use Style I when your intentions are to keep your world running smoothly. To do that you keep most of the intimate information in your Awareness Wheel to yourself, and you eliminate personal or relationship issues from your focus.

When you want to get agreement or compliance, you probably shift to Style II. In Light Control Style you use gentle or tactful persuasive behaviors or appropriate authoritative directives. In Heavy Control Style you use active or passive forcing tactics in disregard of your partner's feelings, wants, and opinions.

When your intention is to explore an issue, you most often use Style III. This style includes many interpretive statements and some action statements, but practically no feeling statements or statements of immediate wants. Style III uses the skills of speaking for self and checking out.

Styles II and III often serve as *transitional* styles. When an issue arises, partners usually move first into Style II which indirectly signals, "I've got an issue." Or they may go into Style III as a way of safely "testing the water" before really getting into the issue. When you are ready to really get down to business, you move to Style IV.

Style IV is distinguished by the intentions to be open, caring, and responsive in your communication. You do this by completely and congruently disclosing your awareness and by tuning into your partner's awareness. You use all the skills we have presented. There is a spirit of sharing and of valuing both yourself and your partner.

MIXED MESSAGES

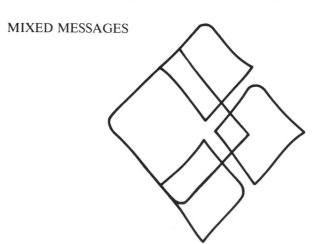

Of the four styles, two are most powerful: Style II and Style IV. These are the two styles used when one or both of you wants to move away from the status quo and change things, or at least seriously consider the possibility of change.

Because Style II is powerful and focuses on change, it can creep into your communication whenever your intentions are mixed. For example, when you want to keep things running smoothly and, at the same time, you want a particular outcome in the discussion, some Style II behaviors often creep into your Style I comments. This will give your partner a *mixed message.*

The same thing can happen with the other styles as well. Your words mostly fit with Style III or Style IV, but the underlying message is a Style II persuasive or forcing message, as in this example: "I don't understand why you don't listen to me." This Style III message is mixed with blame and a closed assumption.

Mixed messages are hard to deal with. Your partner does not know whether to respond to the straight part or to the Style II part. You can best avoid mixed messages by staying aware of your intentions and paying attention to how you express them. Then, when you have intentions from Style II and another style, shift to Style IV and express both of them:

> "I'm really angry with you and I want to blame you for what happened today. It put me in a tough bind."

When you share your feelings and your intention to blame with your partner, everything is out in the open. Then, paradoxically, you stay in Style IV instead of sending mixed messages.

Be careful about one thing, though: just disclosing your intentions and perhaps asking your partner to change does not mean that your partner necessarily will. S/he still has the choice of whether to do what you want or respond in some other way.

Remember, you cannot say to yourself, "I'm going to be in Style IV to change my partner." When you act on this basis, you send a mixed Style IV/II message. But you can say, "I'm going to be in Style IV, change myself and our interaction."

In closing this chapter, we want to note once again that we emphasize Style IV in the Couple Communication program because of its importance in building and maintaining your life together as a couple and because many of you have not had a chance to develop Style IV earlier. However, no single style can be used to effectively communicate all the time. As a flexible, effective communicator you will select the style that matches your intentions.

We invite you to think about your own patterns of using communication styles. Are you mostly a one- or two-style communicator, or do you use all four styles: I, II, III, IV? Where do you use them and with whom? How often do you mix Style II with the other styles? Lastly, which style do you want to work on developing at this time.

KEY IDEAS FROM CHAPTER THREE

1. Effective communicators are flexible.

2. Effective communicators match intention with style.

3. Four communication styles can be identified:

   Style I sociable
   Style II controlling
   Style III searching
   Style IV centered

4. Each style has a useful function.

5. Styles III and IV are most useful for discussing non-routine issues.

6. Indirect, confusing mixed messages happen when Style II is mixed into other styles.

IDENTIFYING COMMUNICATION STYLES   Individual

For each of the statements below, indicate which style you think the statement represents: Style I, II, III, or IV.

                                                                      Answer

1. You know you like it when I kid you about that.   _____

2. How can you do this to me?   _____

3. I'm wondering if the tension between us is because we see so little
    of each other lately.   _____

4. It's about 1200 miles from here to Maine. We can probably make that
    in three days.   _____

5. I'd rather have the apple pie, thanks.   _____

6. I feel pleased about the way we handled that. I was feeling more and
    more frustrated trying to get the thing going, and I could hear you swearing
    under your breath. But during the whole time, neither one of us yelled at
    each other. Wow! I think that's quite an achievement! I just want to let
    you know how good I feel.   _____

7. You're really very good at organizing and managing. You'd probably
    feel more satisfied if you kept track of money and expenses instead of me.
    That way, you'd always feel on top of things and know just where you are. _____

8. I was probably mad at you when you didn't show up.   _____

9. What would happen if we just let things ride for a while?   _____

10. I feel content with where we've gotten so far, so I'd like to stop talking
    about this now and come back to it later tonight.   _____

11. I notice you're wearing a new sweater.   _____

12. I'm avoiding the issue because I'm scared. When we got into a discussion
    about that last week we wound up yelling at each other, and I don't
    want that.   _____

Answers can be found on p. 174

LISTENING TO YOUR VOICE

Individual

Take one of the tapes of yourself and your partner, play it back and listen to *your* own voice. An important part of communication styles is the vocal characteristics used—pitch, tone, rate of speech, etc. So for this exercise, try to forget your words; instead listen to your vocal characteristics for clues to the style(s) you are using. After listening, answer these questions:

a. Is your voice high pitched or low, or does it vary?

b. Is your tone pleasant or harsh? Does it have other tonal qualities?

c. Do you speak rapidly or slowly, or does your rate vary?

d. Do your vocal characteristics change when you shift styles?

Next, apply the Awareness Wheel:

a. Describe how you hear your voice.

b. What interpretations do you make about yourself from what you hear?

c. What feelings do you have as you hear your voice?

LISTENING TO YOUR FIRST TAPE

Individual

Listen to the tape you and your partner made before the program began. Listen for the styles each of you used. Pay particular attention to when you or your partner appeared to use Light Style II to persuade the other to gain agreement. When you tried to persuade, how did your partner respond—defensively, readily agreed, tried to persuade you, or what? When your partner tried to persuade, how did you respond? Identify the styles these responses represent.

DISCUSS AN ISSUE   Individual/Partner

Together with your partner, choose a current concern or issue in your relationship and talk about it, using the self-disclosure skills. Before discussing the issue, however, spend a few minutes organizing your awareness with the Awareness Wheel.

Try to keep your discussion to about ten minutes. Feel free to disclose any awareness you have about the process of your talking together as you discuss the issue.

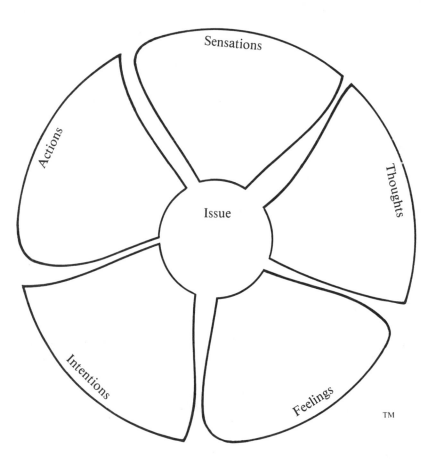

Tape Recording

This exercise is a good one to tape. After you have finished your ten-minute discussion, replay the tape and listen for your use of the skills. Focus on your *own* contribution to the discussion—your use of skills—not on your partner's. You may want to use a Tape Observation Sheet to keep track of your use of the skills.

EXPERIMENTING WITH STYLES: A
Partner

One partner sends a message in any style. Second partner tries to identify the style being used, documenting his/her interpretation. Trade off sending and receiving. Continue until each partner has sent at least two messages in every style.

In this exercise, try not to argue about the "correctness" of an interpretation. Instead, pay particular attention to what you hear (documentation) that leads you to your interpretation. Remember, messages seldom represent a "pure" style.

EXPERIMENTING WITH STYLES: B
Partner

Choose a topic to discuss, then pick a style and have your partner pick a different style. Discuss the topic for a minute or two. Continue this exercise by picking two different styles and discuss the same topic, or a new one, for a minute or two. Repeat this three or four times. Discuss how it feels to be in different styles.

This exercise is designed to help you and your partner practice different styles and heighten your awareness of the different styles. Perhaps you will discover that it's impossible to really deal with and resolve an issue when the two of you are in different styles.

Tape Recording

This is a good exercise to tape record. If you do, discuss your interaction before listening to the tape. Then listen to the tape, paying attention to the styles you and your partner are using, shifts from one style to another, and mixed messages. You may want to use the Styles Observation Sheet to assist you in monitoring your behavior.

CHANGES IN MY LIFE   Partner

Have a discussion of about five minutes in which each of you tells the other about some change occurring in your life. Try to use Style IV to disclose your complete awareness concerning this change and to help your partner disclose his/her complete awareness. As part of your disclosure, you may want to make an action statement to tell your partner about a specific action you will take related to this change. After one partner has described a change, the second partner does the same.

Before doing this exercise, tune into and disclose to your partner your intention(s) for telling him/her about this change—to share, to persuade, to clarify, to demand, etc.

Tape Recording

If you tape your discussion, pay attention to your own use of skills when listening to the tape. All of the self-disclosure skills are appropriate when describing your own change, and the checking-out and shared-meaning skills are appropriate when listening to your partner's change. Both sets of skills are involved in Style IV. You may want to use a Tape Observation Sheet for monitoring your behavior. Sometimes there is a temptation to focus on your partner's behavior. Don't! Keep focused on your own—this is the behavior you can do something about.

WHAT YOU LIKE ABOUT YOUR PARTNER   Partner

Pick something your partner does that you like. Discuss this for about two minutes, using the work styles—Style III and IV. Next, talk about the discussion, using the Awareness Wheel to answer these questions:

1. What were *your* feelings during the discussion?

2. What were *your* intentions toward your partner during the discussion?

3. What actions did *you* take to express these feelings and intentions?

Now trade roles and repeat the exercise and the discussion of your interaction.

Tape Recording

This is a good exercise to tape. When you listen to the tape, look for examples of styles III and IV.

OLD OR NEW ISSUE   Group

1. Without consulting your partner, pick an issue you would like to discuss in front of the group with feedback from other group members and the instructor on your use of skills.

    What is the issue?

2. Now, sit with your partner, compare issues and decide:

    Whose issue you are interested in discussing?

    yours   mine   ours   (circle one)

3. Take a few minutes to reflect on your awareness of the issue. Jot down some key words and phrases to help stimulate more complete awareness.

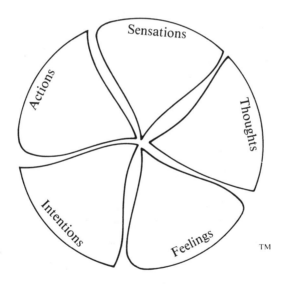

4. When your turn comes to discuss the issue with your partner, try to use Style IV to share complete and congruent awareness about the issue. Be careful not to make a long speech about your awareness—just exchange it with your partner. In the time available you will probably not be able to resolve the issue, but both of you will be able to share a good deal of your awareness.

PROGRESS REVIEW

Here's another exercise to help you monitor your progress in learning the skills, processes, and frameworks presented in the first three chapters. Place an X in the appropriate box to indicate how you rate your learning of each skill, process, and framework.

	Initial Learning	Awkward Use	Conscious Application	Natural Use
SKILLS				
Speaking for self				
Making sense statements				
Making interpretive statements				
Making feeling statements				
Making intention statements				
Making action statements				
Attentive listening and observing				
Encouraging/inviting disclosure				
Checking out				
PROCESSES				
Documenting interpretations				
Shared meaning process				
Setting procedures				
Flexibility in using styles				
FRAMEWORKS				
Awareness Wheel				
Focus of Conversation				
Styles framework				

Note: By this point, you may have recognized that some of your communication patterns are not what you would like them to be. For example, you may have discovered that you use Style II communication more often than you like. If this is the case, we hope you will be pleased that you have learned this about yourself. You can change your patterns if you are dissatisfied with them.

TAPE OBSERVATION SHEET

You might want to use this form in listening to tapes of exercises. Focus on your own behavior and jot down words or phrases illustrating your use of specific behaviors or skills.

Tape 1	Tape 2
Speaking for self	
Documenting interpretations	
Making feeling statements	
Making intention statements	
Making action statements	
Checking out	
Shared meaning process	

STYLES OBSERVATION SHEET

You might want to use this form in listening to tapes of exercises. Focus on your own behavior and jot down words or phrases illustrating your use of various styles.

Tape 1	Tape 2
Style I	
Style II	
Style III	
Style IV	
Mixed Messages	

GROUP OBSERVATION SHEET

As partners talk together in front of the group, use the spaces below to document your observation of the styles they use. Pick *one* style to watch for and write it down in the space provided. Then write the names of the partners you will be observing. During their discussion, jot down words or phrases which document their use of the style.

Style:
Names:_____ _____

Style:
Names:_____ _____

Style:
Names:_____ _____

Style:
Names:_____ _____

Style:
Names:_____ _____

Style:
Names:_____ _____

ESTEEM BUILDING

CHAPTER 4

COUNTING YOURSELF AND YOUR PARTNER

Couple Communication presents some very useful tools for communicating with your partner. But there's a special feature about tools we want you to note: any tools, including these, can be used to build or to tear down. You can use these communication skills and ideas to be more genuine with your partner or to con him/her, to share more of yourself or to keep yourself hidden, to improve your relationship or to destroy it.

In this chapter we want to provide you with one more tool. You can use it like a compass to check on whether you are using your skills to head in the direction you really want to go. We call this tool the counting framework. It is a framework you can use to examine whether you are communicating in a way that says, "I count me and I count you," or not.

Notice how we phrased this: "I count me and I count you." The focus is on what *I do,* not on what you do. What I do toward myself and toward you depends on how I value myself and how I value you. These attitudes of valuing are the key.

When you talk with your partner, what you say and how you say it tell a great deal about your attitude toward both your partner and yourself. For example, when you listen attentively to your partner, you indicate to him/her: I count you. You also indicate this when you ask your partner what is in his/her Awareness Wheel, when you document your interpretation of something s/he said, and when you share a meaning. When you clearly state what you want for yourself or what you are feeling, it is a way of saying: I count myself.

How you talk with others does not just reflect your attitude toward yourself and your partner. The underlying value you place on yourself and on your partner—your counting attitude—has a powerful impact on the way you communicate, shaping your use of your Awareness Wheel and the communication skills.

When you value or count someone—yourself or another person—you express a positive set of assumptions about that person's significance:

—faith in the intention to treat each person as important,

—confidence in the ability to handle situations, or to recognize when help is needed,

—trust in the willingness to follow through on promises,

—belief in the commitment to each person's well-being.

On the other hand, when you discount someone—including yourself —the set of assumptions is just the opposite: lack of faith, confidence, trust, and belief.

How important is your counting attitude? We think the foundation of your relationship with your partner lies in the attitudes each of you holds about yourself and each other. We think it is *that* important. The tough part is to be able to feel angry or disappointed with yourself or your partner and still count both of you in the process.

SELF-CONCEPT AND SELF-ESTEEM

Your self-esteem grows out of your self-concept in this way: you have a mental "picture" of yourself. If you look closely, you find that it is not a single picture. Instead, it includes both snapshots and movies. It shows you alone by yourself and interacting with others. It shows you from times in the past and present, as well as in the imagined future.

You will probably note some variety in the scenes. Depending on time, place, situation, and who you are with, you are somewhat different. Some of your characteristics seem to stand out more than others, though, and some patterns of action seem to be repeated more than others. This overall process of picturing yourself we refer to as your *self-concept.*

Accompanying these pictures of yourself is an accumulated set of evaluations and judgments: successful, unsuccessful, competent, incompetent, loving, unloving, and many more. Add to these an accumulated set of feelings about yourself: admiration, shame, confidence, warmth, hope, guilt, pleasure, etc. This set of evaluations, judgments, and feelings makes up your self-worth, your *self-esteem*. Some of these evaluations and feelings seem to stand out more than others, and often they are consistent. That's why we say one person has high self-esteem (approves and feels good about him/herself most of the time) and another has low self-esteem (usually disapproves and feels bad about him/herself).

What we find for most people, then, is a relatively stable self-concept accompanied by a relatively stable sense of self-worth. But even though they are fairly stable, your self-concept and self-esteem are not cast in bronze. They are the names for dynamic, continuously developing and changing processes which involve all dimensions of your Awareness Wheel, including your current actions and intentions. Because of this, people who have high self-esteem occasionally experience pretty negative feelings about themselves. The same is true in reverse: people with low self-esteem sometimes feel good about themselves.

We mention this because it is not just your general level of self-esteem that affects how you talk. Your more momentary view of yourself has impact too. When you are down on yourself, it can be difficult to act in ways that count yourself. Even then, however, you do have a choice: you can act in ways which say, "I count myself," or in ways which say, "I don't count myself."

The reason you always have a choice is this: your counting attitude is not the same as your feelings, your momentary view of yourself, or even your more stable and enduring self-esteem. None of these is the key. Instead, the key is whether you treat yourself as significant, as someone whose intentions, thoughts, feelings, etc., are worth taking into account. The same thing is true about counting your partner. Your counting attitude is based on whether you treat him/her as significant, not on your current feelings toward or momentary view of him/her. You can act in ways that count others even when you dislike them.

Your counting attitude seems to grow out of a deeper belief in the fundamental value of every person. For many people this enduring belief is based on a respect for the integrity of each person as one of God's unique creations. For others the belief is based on a different value system. But whatever the source of the belief, it underlies your counting attitude and makes it possible for you to say, "I count myself," even when things are at their lowest ebb for you.

COUNTING SELF AND PARTNER

You can express counting attitudes in many different ways. The behaviors you use to count yourself and your partner revolve around how you treat your own and your partner's Awareness Wheels and decisions. Specific behaviors that show you count—or don't count—yourself and your partner are these:

I Count Me

—as I actively tune into my own experience and fill out my Awareness Wheel.

—as I accept my awareness of who I am, owning my thoughts, feelings, actions, and intentions even when I find them unpleasant.

—as I disclose all parts of my Awareness Wheel when appropriate to do so.

—as I accept responsibility for my own decisions and actions.

I Don't Count Me

—when I disregard my self-awareness.

—when I do not fully accept my experience.

—when I do not disclose from my Awareness Wheel when it is appropriate to do so.

—when I do not accept responsibility for my own decisions and actions.

I Count You

—as I pay attention to you, to your expressions of your awareness.

—as I respect and acknowledge your thoughts, feelings, and intentions as your own, even if I disagree with them or find them unpleasant.

—as I invite and encourage you to express your self-awareness when appropriate.

—as I leave room for you to accept responsibility for your own decisions and actions.

—as I act in ways that demonstrate caring for you and enjoying you.

—as I leave room for and even demonstrate appreciation for our differences.

—as I provide feedback that can be useful to you.

I Don't Count You

—when I ignore your Awareness Wheel or refuse to accept or acknowledge your experience as your own.

—when I deny real differences between us or insist that you be just like me.

—when I try to take responsibility for your decisions and actions.

—when I act in ways that demonstrate not caring for you.

—when I avoid providing you with useful feedback.

Now that you have some familiarity with ways to count yourself and your partner, we would like you to think about your own life. Recall a recent situation in which you counted your partner:

Where were you? (home, with friends, etc.)

How did you feel?

What did you do or say to show that s/he counted?

Next, recall a situation in which you counted yourself:

Where were you?

How did you feel?

What did you do or say to show that you counted yourself?

We hope some counting situations came readily to mind. If not, pay. more attention to counting yourself and your partner. Showing your partner directly that you value him/her helps develop a more positive climate in your relationship. If you would like to appreciate your partner more, then act in ways which show appreciation. If you would like to feel more caring toward him/her, then find ways to express caring.

Your feelings about yourself also are affected by whether you act in ways that say "I count me," or "I don't count me." The clues you give off about how you value yourself influence how others value you, which reinforces your original self-esteem, and so on ad infinitum. Let's look at contrasting examples of messages from two different people:

> (vibrant, buoyant manner) "I think I just had a good idea! I want to tell you about it!"

> (monotone, unenthusiastic) "I had an idea about that, not that it's anything special. Let me see if I can remember it now."

What kind of esteem messages is each communicating about self? And which of the two is more likely to receive close attention, i.e., a message back from the listener that says, "I value what you have to say?"

COMBINATIONS: COUNTING/NOT COUNTING SELF AND PARTNER

In any dialogue with your partner, your statements carry messages about esteem of self *and* esteem of partner. Of course, sometimes the esteem elements are not easy to spot. Other times they are obvious, as in this example, "You'll never figure it out. Here, I'll show you how to do it." This statement clearly conveys that, "I count me and I don't count you." When you combine counting attitudes toward yourself and your partner, you will find there are four possible combinations. We think you will find it helpful to notice which combination you are expressing at times, especially when you and your partner have an issue to deal with or a difference to resolve. Let's examine each of these combinations.

I DON'T COUNT ME/I DON'T COUNT YOU

Here I treat both of us as being not very worthwhile. This combination is characterized by feelings of hopelessness or despair, because I am acting as if neither one of us can take charge of him/herself and direct his/her own course of action responsibly.

My messages may contain Heavy Style II put-downs of both myself and my partner; or I may devalue myself and him/her in indirect ways, for example, with noncommital or complaining messages (Style I/II or III/II mixed messages). Or I may give the impression that I'm leaving our destiny to chance or hoping for some outside authority to give us direction. Here is an example:

> "Neither of us can change. We're just stuck with each other the way we are. All we can do is make the best of it."

I COUNT ME/I DON'T COUNT YOU

When you find yourself using this combination, you probably define the situation as one in which one person is right and the other wrong, or one wins and the other loses. In effect you are saying, "Since only one of us can be valued in this situation, I'll be the one!'' You are probably trying to control the outcome of the situation at the expense of both your partner and your relationship. You overemphasize your own Awareness Wheel and pay little attention to your partner's.

This combination comes across as selfish and demanding. It is usually expressed with Heavy Style II—labeling, blaming, defending, or concealing. These Style II messages frequently result in similar responses from your partner. Most arguments involve the trading back and forth of I count/I don't count you messages by both partners:

> "Why in the heck did you say that in front of him? I'm not that way, and you know he'll use it against me sometime!"

> "If you don't want me to say things like that about you, then change!"

In this short dialogue, both partners are making presumptions about the other, demanding something from the other, and claiming that, "I'm right." It is obvious they are not going to get very far in resolving the issue; in fact, they probably will not even be able to identify what the issue is.

I DON'T COUNT ME/I COUNT YOU

In this combination, I depreciate myself while attempting to please and placate my partner. I devalue myself and value my partner. In this combination I'm wrong and my partner is right; my partner is important and I'm not. I pay close attention to my partner's Awareness Wheel and ignore my own. I may use a Heavy Style II message to put myself down; but more often, this combination uses mixed messages in Style I/II or III/II.

> A: "I'm concerned about how we make decisions. When we started talking about how we might reduce expenses, I heard your voice getting loud and I thought I was being blamed. I felt angry and frustrated that nothing was resolved. I'd like to talk about how we might handle it differently."

B: "Well, you're right, and I'm really sorry about it. I get so frustrated, I just lose control. I can't seem to stop myself from doing this. Maybe it would be better if you just made these decisions. You know you make good decisions and this would keep these silly arguments from happening."

Here B uses Style III/II to put him/herself down and, at the same time, build A up. But s/he does so in such a way that s/he tries to shift responsibility to A for both making the decisions and keeping B from blowing up. How do you suppose A would feel about that?

Adopting the I don't count/I count you combination involves a contradiction: when you do this, you really discount your partner, too. For example, when you put yourself down and try to shift responsibility to your partner, as B did, you fail to acknowledge his/her right to not be responsible for you. When you try to placate your partner, you say, in effect, that s/he is too fragile or unstable to level with and you discount him/her in that way. Or if you act the martyr, you convey a message that your partner wanted you to humble yourself; this message implies s/he does not care about you very much. The next time someone behaves toward you in a demeaning, placating, or martyring way, be aware of your feeling response. You will probably feel irritated or annoyed.

The three combinations described so far all have in common the effect of preventing you and your partner from talking honestly and productively with each other because:

—they interfere with your getting down to brass tacks around important issues, either directly or indirectly;

—they fail to convey respect and fail to acknowledge awareness of self and awareness of partner;

—if you attempt to count only one partner—yourself or your partner—your objective is to manipulate rather than understand.

Now let's turn to a winning combination.

I COUNT ME/I COUNT YOU

In this combination, you are tuned in to yourself and accept your awareness. And you are also alert to your partner and accept his/her self-disclosures. You demonstrate commitment to your own well-being, and to your partner's well being as well. If your partner is acting on the same intentions, too, then together you can face issues and conflicts directly with confidence, and you can find solutions acceptable to both of you. You are not leaving your destiny to chance. You have hope that you can work things out.

If you are dealing with a meaningful issue holding this attitude, you will be using Styles IV and III in combination, or just Style IV as in this example:

> "I'm anxious to move, but I'm worried about all the changes it represents. I'd like to talk about it with you."

> "I'm relieved to hear I'm not the only one of us who's worrying about it. I'd like to try to figure out together just what we're in for."

When there is not an issue, I count/I count you is often expressed in play and in sociable "rapping" or chit-chat. Sometimes, positive spontaneous Style II statements also have a way of saying I count/I count you, such as "We're great!"

What we have been emphasizing so far is that the attitudes you hold toward yourself and your partner have a big effect on the messages you send. However, it is not easy to identify exactly what a person's attitude toward him/herself and toward his/her partner is by listening to a single message. That is because most messages express an attitude about only self or only partner, not both. If you want to identify your own attitudes toward self and other, or your partner's attitudes, it is often necessary to pay attention to statements that are made over a period of time.

CHOOSING TO COUNT YOURSELF AND YOUR PARTNER

Earlier in the chapter, we pointed out that you always have a choice about whether to count or discount yourself and your·partner. Even when things are tough, you can make the choice to count yourself and count your partner.We would like to return to this point here by illustrating a sequence of choices you have because we think the point is so important.

Let's listen to a conversation between partners A and B as they confront a minor crisis. A and B were looking forward to an evening out together. At the last minute, they discovered that neither had arranged for a sitter to stay with their children.

CHOICE POINT ONE

Partner A begins the conversation. Here is what A's inner awareness looks like:

I'm awfully disappointed. I was looking forward to this evening.
I thought you would arrange for the sitter. I wonder who goofed.
I wish I had checked earlier.

At this first step, A could respond in any of the four counting combinations. Here are some different responses A could use:

I don't count/I don't count you; "Nothing goes right anymore! We just can't get it together." (Speaks for other and doesn't speak for self; no acknowledgement of own or other's feelings.)

I count/I don't count you; "I'm disappointed! You know it was your turn to get the sitter." (Counts own feelings; speaks for other and blames.)

I don't count/I count you; "I expect this is pretty disappointing for you. I'm sorry I wrecked your evening." (Counts other's feelings; suppresses own feelings and thoughts.)

I count/I count you; "I'm so disappointed, and I'll bet you are too. It looks like each of us thought it was the other's turn. I wish I had checked it with you." (Counts both own and other's feelings; tells own thoughts and feelings without blaming.)

CHOICE POINT TWO

Let's assume that A chose the I count/I don't count you response: "I'm disappointed! You know it was your turn to get the sitter." Here is B's awareness as s/he prepares to respond:

> I'm awfully disappointed. I was looking forward to this evening. I thought you would arrange for the babysitter, but I hear you blaming me. I hate being blamed! I wish I had checked on this earlier. I'm getting mad, but I still wish we could have some fun together.

Partner B still can choose a response to express any counting combination. Here are some different responses B could use:

> *I don't count/I don't count you;* "How do you think I feel? I don't know why we even bother trying to go out. It never works out." (Does not tell own feelings and intentions; expresses helpless feeling about self and partner.)

> *I count/I don't count you;* "My turn! Don't give me that! I got the sitter last time." (Defends self and counter attacks; fails to acknowledge other's feelings.)

> *I don't count/I count you;* "I'm sorry. I know how disappointed you are. I should have checked with you." (Blames self; acknowledges partner's feelings and ignores own.)

> *I count/I count you;* "My turn! I got the sitter last time. I'm disappointed too, and mad at both of us for not checking. Maybe we can still find someone. I'd like to try. How about you?" (Defends self; acknowledges both own and partner's feelings; treats their wants as important by offering to search for alternatives; checks out partner's view.)

CHOICE POINT THREE

Let's assume that B responded to A by choosing the I count/I don't count you response: "My turn! Don't give me that! I got the sitter last time." A and B are well on their way toward a big fight. Here is A's awareness at this point:

> I hate being blamed! I'm mad at B. I'm afraid it may be too late to save the evening. I'm sad that our evening is turning out like this. I'd like to have some fun tonight.

Even though A and B have traded harsh accusations, and even though A is now quite angry at B, A still can choose any of the four counting combinations. Here are examples of each:

> *I don't count/I don't count you;* "There's no point in discussing it

further!'' (Speaks for no one; acknowledges no one's feelings, thoughts and wants; indicates both are helpless.)

I count/I don't count you; "If you were counting on me to get the sitter, you might have said something. I was really looking forward to this evening. Now you've ruined it.'' (Defends self by shifting blame; acknowledges own wants but not partner's; blames directly.)

I don't count/I count you; "I'm sorry. What do you think we should do now?'' (Indicates acceptance of blame but denies own awareness; acts helpless.)

I count/I count you; "I'm sorry I blamed you. I'm mad at you and me both because I'm disappointed. I'd still like to have some fun. What about you?'' (Acknowledges partner's feelings about being blamed and reports own feelings; speaks for self; focuses on immediate wants in situation; checks out partner's view)

Both count messages can be difficult to send, especially when you and your partner are arguing, as A and B were. You may find it hard to stay with the I count/I count you combination when you are feeling hurt or angry. But try to adopt this attitude and use communication skills to stay away from messages which blame or demand·change in your partner. It is especially important to keep tuned in to your intentions, acknowledge them and act on them:

—What do you want for yourself, immediately and long range?

—What do you want for your partner, immediately and long range?

Even if a disagreement does not involve a fight, there is still a temptation to shift from an intention to understand to an intention to win. This may lead to an I count/I don't count you combination, usually expressed with a Heavy Style II or with mixed messages. To maintain a both-count combination, all of the skills presented earlier in the book are relevant and helpful. For example, documenting impressions or conclusions with sensory data requires real effort on my part, an effort to put my partner in the picture. This says to him/her, "You count to me." Asking my partner to share a meaning says that I treat both my message and his/her understanding of it as being important—we both count.

In closing this chapter, we would like to remind you one last time that you always have a choice. Even when a disagreement is serious and feelings are strong, each of you has a choice about counting yourself and about counting your partner. You can each choose to count only yourself and create a fight. Or you can each choose to count both yourself and your partner and create a context for developing understanding and mutual satisfaction. The counting choices the two of you make create the situation and go a long way toward determining the outcome of your discussion.

KEY IDEAS FROM CHAPTER 4

1. Both skills and spirit are important in communication.

2. Your counting attitudes express the spirit of your communication and have a major impact on how you talk.

3. You can either count or discount yourself and your partner.

4. Counting attitudes come in combinations.

5. Expressing an I count/I count you attitude helps build your own esteem, your partner,'s esteem, and your relationship together.

6. Even when you are down, you can choose to count yourself and your partner.

COUNTING QUIZ   Individual

For each of the statements below, indicate which counting attitude you think the statement represents: (a) I don't count/I don't count you; (b) I count/I don't count you; (c) I don't count/I count you; (d) I count/I count you.

	Answer

1. You sure are good to me—I don't know what I would do without you. _____

2. You should go; you'll have fun. _____

3. I'm glad we talked that over. I understand you better and I think you understand me better too. _____

4. Let me tell you how I feel, and don't interrupt like you usually do. _____

5. I need some advice but I'm afraid you won't be able to help. I think this problem will be too tough for both of us. _____

6. I really don't care what we do. Anything you decide is all right with me. _____

7. I'd like to try that. What do you think? _____

8. I don't like the way you treated her, but maybe you had a reason. I'd like to know what you were trying to do. _____

9. I don't think either of us wants to work this out, and even if we do, it won't make any difference. _____

10. My first reaction was to say, "I'll do it." But after I thought about it for awhile, I knew I couldn't. I think we could do it if we worked together, though. Would you be willing to help me? _____

11. That sounds like fun. I'd like to come along, but I'm sure I'd be a drag on you. _____

12. Can't you do it? It's easy. You should be able to do it without any trouble. _____

Answers can be found on p. 174

ESTEEM BUILDING   Individual

Think back to the last day or two and write down things you said or things you did which counted yourself and did not count yourself. Do the same for counting or not counting your partner.

Examples of counting self   Examples of counting partner

1.   1.

2.   2.

3.   3.

4.   4.

Examples of not counting self   Examples of not counting partner

1.   1.

2.   2.

3.   3.

4.   4.

DISCUSS AN ISSUE   Partner

Pick an issue of importance to your relationship which you and your partner are in conflict about. Try to resolve the issue with both you and your partner sending mutual I count/I count you messages using your complete and congruent Awareness Wheels. Discuss the issue for about ten minutes. If you cannot resolve it in this time-frame, stop, leave the issue, come back to it later.

Before discussing the issue, spend a few minutes organizing your awareness about the issue in the Awareness Wheel.

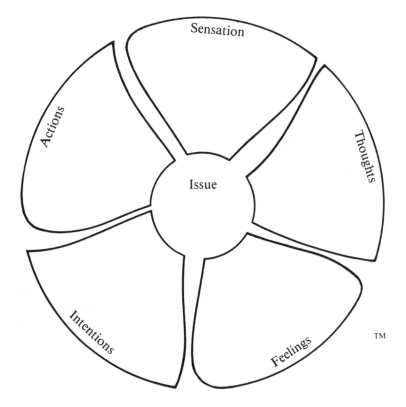

After you have finished, use the Awareness Wheel to review your awareness *during the discussion.*

Tape Recording

This is a good exercise to tape. When you listen, pay attention to your own messages, particularly your use of the self-disclosure skills and whether you stayed in, or shifted out of, an I count/I count you attitude. You may want to use the Counting Observation Sheet to monitor your behavior.

SHARING YOURSELF   Partner

You can combine the I count/I count you attitude with the self-disclosure skills by consciously using them in sharing yourself with your partner. Share something about yourself with your partner: an experience in your day; a reflection on the past; hopes and dreams for the future; appreciation of your partner. Try to maintain an I count/I count you attitude throughout. Reverse roles and repeat.

CRITICAL FEEDBACK   Partner

Give your partner one—and only one—piece of *critical feedback.* In your feedback, make sure you document your criticism. Try to maintain an I count/I count you attitude as you give the feedback. Partner then reflects back your message and shared meaning continues until message sent equals message received. Partner then shares his/her awareness regarding your criticism.

Next, reverse roles and repeat the process. Stop exercise after one criticism by each partner.

Tape Recording

This is a good exercise to tape. As you listen to the tape, pay attention to your own communication, looking particularly for instances when you may have shifted from an I count/I count you position. If you did shift, note your partner's response. You may want to use the Counting Observation Sheet to help monitor your behavior.

WHAT YOU LIKE ABOUT YOURSELF AND YOUR PARTNER   Partner

For two or three minutes, disclose to your partner things you like about *yourself*—try not to either qualify or disqualify your statements. Next, partner reports back what s/he understands, sharing a meaning with you about things you like about yourself. Then partner tells you for two or three minutes things s/he likes about *you,* followed by sharing a meaning about his/her message.

After this process is completed, reverse roles and repeat.

BEFORE AND AFTER   Partner

Repeat the audio tape exercise you and your partner did before you began Couple Communication I. Turn to the introduction for a description of the exercise.

Tape Recording

After completing the two five-minute discussions, listen to both your "before" and "after" tapes, paying particular attention to how you changed—or did not change—in your use of communication skills. Focus on your own contribution to the discussions, using a Tape Observation Sheet.

SELF/OTHER ESTEEM   Group

This exercise involves two phases. First, separately complete the self- and other-esteem framework. Second, share your perceptions with your partner.

1. Begin by filling in a specific time period you are thinking about. Next, list issues in your relationship with your partner that you think you have approached from each of the counting attitudes; jot down words or phrases to document your expression of this attitude. At this point, do *not* fill in anything under the column labeled "action plan."

Self- and Other-Esteem Framework

Time Period   (week, month, etc.)

Counting Attitude	Self	Partner	Issues	Documentation	Action Plan
I Don't Count Me/ I Don't Count You					
I Count Me/ I Don't Count You					
I Don't Count Me/ I Count You					
I Count Me/ I Count You					

2. Share your perceptions with your partner, paying particular attention to the counting attitudes the two of you express in dealing with the same issues. Next, under "action plan," jot down notes on how you will go about changing your pattern of interaction around an issue, if you want to change it.

OLD OR NEW ISSUE   Group

1. Without consulting your partner, pick an issue you would like to discuss in front of the group with feedback from other group members and the instructor on your use of skills.

   What is the issue?

2. Now, sit with your partner, compare issues and decide:

   Whose issue are you interested in discussing?

   yours   mine   ours   (circle one)

3. If you are going to practice discussing an issue in group with skill feedback, take a few minutes to reflect on your awareness of the issue. Jot down some key words and phrases to help stimulate more complete awareness.

4. When your turn comes to discuss the issue with your partner, try to use an I count/I count you attitude as you share your complete and congruent awareness about the issue. Be careful not to make a long speech about your awareness—just exchange it with your partner. In the time available you will probably not be able to resolve the issue, but both of you will be able to share a good deal of your awareness.

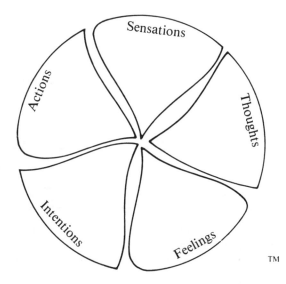

PROGRESS REVIEW

This exercise gives you a chance to assess your progress in learning all the skills, processes, and frameworks taught in Couple Communication I. Place an X in the appropriate box to indicate your learning of each skill, process, and framework.

	Initial Learning	Awkward Use	Conscious Application	Natural Use
SKILLS				
Speaking for self				
Making sense statements				
Making interpretive statements				
Making feeling statements				
Making intention statements				
Making action statements				
Attentive listening and observing				
Encouraging/inviting disclosure				
Checking out				
PROCESSES				
Documenting interpretations				
Shared meaning process				
Setting procedures				
Flexibility in using styles				
Maintaining an I count/ I count you posture				
FRAMEWORKS				
Awareness Wheel				
Styles framework				
I count/I count you framework				

Note: If you haven't reached the natural use stage for each skill, process, and framework, this is normal. Skill learning takes considerable practice and a long time. Continued use of the skills in your daily life, combined with further use of exercises in this book, will help you improve and refine your skills.

TAPE OBSERVATION SHEET

You might want to use this form in listening to tapes of exercises. Focus on your own behavior and jot down words or phrases illustrating your use of specific behaviors or skills.

Tape 1	Tape 2
Speaking for self	
Documenting interpretations	
Making feeling statements	
Making intention statements	
Making action statements	
Attentive listening and observing	
Encouraging/inviting disclosure	
Checking out	
Shared meaning process	

COUNTING OBSERVATION SHEET

You might want to use this form in listening to tapes of exercises. Focus on your own behavior and jot down words or phrases illustrating your use of various counting attitudes.

Tape 1	Tape 2
I don't count/I don't count you	
I count/I don't count you	
I don't count/I count you	
I count/I count you	

GROUP OBSERVATION SHEET

As partners talk together in front of the group, use the spaces below to document your observations. Pick *one* counting attitude to watch for and write it down in the space provided. Then write the names of the partners you will be observing. During their discussion, jot down words or phrases which document their use of the counting attitude.

Counting Attitude:
Names:_____ _____

Counting Attitude:
Names:_____ _____

Counting Attitude:
Names:_____ _____

Counting Attitude:
Names:_____ _____

Counting Attitude:
Names:_____ _____

Counting Attitude:
Names:_____ _____

EPILOGUE

WHERE CAN YOU GO FROM HERE?

How have you done? What have you learned? How are you using the frameworks and skills? Which ones are particularly useful to you? Are you using the skills with others besides your partner?

We hope your answers to these questions are positive, and we hope you are moving well along toward the natural-use phase with the skills. We also hope you will continue practicing and using the skills and frameworks regularly so you can keep making progress. When you and your partner are able to use the skills naturally, the two of you can realize even greater benefits from these communication tools.

In closing *Talking Together*, we would like to give you information about where you can go from here to continue developing your communication abilities and, more important, developing your relationship with your partner. We will describe additional resources available for these purposes. You can request further information about those supplied through Interpersonal Communication Programs by filling out the last page of this book and returning it to us. Other resources discussed are available in your local community.

REVIEW AND REINFORCE SKILLS WITH AUDIO CASSETTE TAPES

Like anything you learn, the more you use your interpersonal communication skills, the more they will become a natural part of you. To help reinforce your learning after participating in a CC group, an audio cassette tape series is available, entitled *Communication Skills for Couples*. Each tape uses couples' real discussion to illustrate the principles and skills taught in CC.

Tape I-A reviews four styles of talking, and Tape I-B focuses on using your Awareness Wheel. Tape II-A describes and illustrates the attentive listening skills. Tape II-B introduces you to a new way of using your Awarness Wheel to make decisions, what we call Mapping An Issue. This is an exciting new process for using your own and your partner's awareness to resolve issues and make more satisfying decisions together.

The cassettes series contains: two audio cassette tapes with 20 minutes of material per side; easy-to-follow Listener's Guide for couples and group programming; Talking Together (optional); and an attractive protective binder with materials pocket.

A special edition of the tape series, which includes inspirational scriptures on communication, is also available for Christian couples. When inquiring about the tape series, please indicate which edition you prefer.

COUPLE COMMUNICATION II

A second direction for you to go is to participate in Couple Communication II. This advanced program builds on the foundation established in CCI. Besides giving you more skill practice, it takes the basic tools—the Awareness Wheel and communication skills—and teaches you how to systematically "map issues" and handle the many kinds of concerns and decisions the two of you will face in your life together.

CC II also helps you look at the broader patterns in your relationship. It introduces several frameworks to give you perspective on the bigger picture of your lives individually and as a couple.

The text for CC II is, *STRAIGHT TALK: A New Way To Get Closer To Others By Saying What You Really Mean* by Sherod Miller, Daniel Wackman, Elam Nunnally and Carol Saline. Be sure to ask your instructors when they will be offering CC II.

BECOME A COUPLE COMMUNICATION INSTRUCTOR

Another direction you might consider after completing Couple Communication is to teach other couples what you have learned. If you are interested, write or call ICP (see Information Request Form on the last page of *TALKING TOGETHER*) for information about obtaining CC instructor materials specifically designed to enable you to lead CC groups.

Teaching Couple Communication can be a fulfilling experience for you and your partner, and it can have several specific benefits as well:

—help you and your partner really learn the material,
—give you and your partner something interesting and stimulating to do together.
—give the two of you a chance to meet and help other couples.

UNDERSTANDING US

If you are interested in an enjoyable learning experience with your whole family, ask your CC instructors when they will be offering the Understanding Us Program.

Understanding Us helps any family—two parent, single-parent, and step-parent—view their lives together as a system maintaining stability and initiating change across stages of development. To do this, Understanding Us teaches two major frameworks. The Family Map provides a way for each family to learn about its adaptability and cohesiveness as a group. The Identity Cycle gives each family member a look at how s/he is constantly changing and the impact these changes have on the family as a whole.

Eight to twelve families (members 6 years and older) meet for four two-hour sessions with an Understanding Us instructor. Exercises usually involve families as units, but some exercises mix members from different families or join two families together. Throughout the course, families explore their system's rules, roles, roots and rituals as a way of increasing their understanding, appreciation and enjoyment of their uniqueness. Additional exercises between sessions, as well as reading from the program text, *UNDERSTANDING US: Family Development I* by Dr. Patrick Carnes, add depth to each family's learning.

OTHER EXPERIENCES

Interpersonal Communication Programs is not the only organization which offers programs for couples and families. Many churches and community centers do so as well, ranging from one-night programs to weekend retreats to regular monthly meetings. You might wish to inquire at various places in your community about the type and availability of programs they offer.

Another organization offering experiences for couples is the Association of Couples for Marriage Enrichment. ACME has chapters in many locations. Typically, the chapters hold meetings once a month and provide a chance for couples to get together to share experiences, participate in workshops, listen to speakers, and the like. ACME groups also hold weekend retreats. For the name and address of an ACME contact person in your area, write to:

> ACME
> 459 South Church Street
> P.O. Box 10596
> Winston-Salem, North Carolina 27108

Finally, whether you are interested in any of the things mentioned here or not, drop us a note to tell us about your experiences with Couple Communication. We enjoy hearing from you.

ANSWERS TO QUIZZES

Answers to Self-Disclosure Quiz: 1-D; 2-C; 3-B; 4-C; 6-E; 7-A; 8-B; 9-E; 10-C; 11-D; 12-A; 13-D; 14-E; 15-A.

Answers to Styles Quiz: 1-II; 2-II; 3-III; 4-I; 5-I; 6-IV; 7-II; 8-III; 9-III; 10-IV; 11-I; 12-IV.

Answers to Counting Attitude Quiz: 1-C; 2-B; 3D; 4-B; 5-A; 6-C; 7-D; 8-D; 9-A; 10-D; 11-C; 12-B.

INFORMATION REQUEST FORM

Please send me the following information (check all that apply):

☐ Name(s) of Certified Couple Communication instructors in my area.

☐ Information about Couple Communication Instructor Materials.

☐ Information about Understanding Us Instructor Materials.

Name _____

Address _____

City and State _____ Zip _____

OCCUPATION _____

Return to: Interpersonal Communication Programs
7201 South Broadway
Littleton, Colorado 80122

BOOK ORDER

If you would like to order any of the books published by Interpersonal Communication Programs, please fill in the appropriate information below and return this form with payment:

	Price	Quantity	Amount
Couple Communication I: Talking Together	$11.95	_____	_____
Audio Cassette Series without *Talking Together**	$24.95	_____	_____
Audio Cassette Series with *Talking Together**	$29.95	_____	_____
Connecting with Self and Others	$12.95	_____	_____
Connecting Skills Workbook	$11.95	_____	_____
Understanding Us: Family Development I	$11.95	_____	_____
Working Together	$34.95	_____	_____

*A special edition which include inspirational scriptures on communication for Christian couples is also available. Please check if you wish to order the Christian edition.

Charges for Postage and Handling
Total Order

$	.00-25.00	3.00
	25.01-50.00	4.00
	50.01-100.00	5.00
	over 100.00,	5% of Total

CO residents add 3.6% sales tax _____

Postage/Handling _____

TOTAL AMOUNT PAYABLE _____

Payment must accompany order. Make checks payable to:
INTERPERSONAL COMMUNICATION PROGRAMS